Balancing the Regulation and Taxation of Banking

Balancing the Regulation and Taxation of Banking

Sajid M. Chaudhry
School of Management, Swansea University, UK

Andrew W. Mullineux
Business School, University of Birmingham, UK

Natasha Agarwal
Indian Institute of Foreign Trade, New Delhi, India

Edward Elgar
PUBLISHING

Cheltenham, UK • Northampton, MA, USA

Published by
Edward Elgar Publishing Limited
The Lypiatts
15 Lansdown Road
Cheltenham
Glos GL50 2JA
UK

Edward Elgar Publishing, Inc.
William Pratt House
9 Dewey Court
Northampton
Massachusetts 01060
USA

A catalogue record for this book
is available from the British Library

Library of Congress Control Number: 2015938873

This book is available electronically in the **Elgar**online
Economics subject collection
DOI 10.4337/9781785360275

ISBN 978 1 78536 026 8 (cased)
ISBN 978 1 78536 027 5 (eBook)

Typeset by Columns Design XML Ltd, Reading
Printed and bound in Great Britain by T.J. International Ltd, Padstow

Contents

Tables

Acknowledgements

This is the Report from the 'Taxing Banks Fairly' workstream (led by Co-Investigator Professor Andy Mullineux, on which Dr Sajid Mukhtar Chaudhry was employed as a postdoc Research Fellow from 1 November 2012 to 31 October 2013) of the Arts and Humanities Research Council-funded 'FinCris' Project, Reference Number: AH/J001252/1 (http://fincris.net/).

1. Introduction

Since the 'Global, or Great, Financial Crisis' (GFC) of 2007–2009, policy makers and regulators have been seeking the best approach to 'taxing' financial institutions and their activities in the financial markets. There are a number of ways of taxing banks, with the goals of improving their stability, and dissuading them from engaging in overly risky activities while also raising tax revenue. One way is through regulations and another is through imposing direct 'fiscal' taxes that raise revenues. Hitherto, regulations have been the dominant approach to ensuring the stability of banks and the banking sector. The post-crisis Basel III framework strengthens the minimum risk-related capital requirements outlined in Basel I and Basel II and also introduces new regulations in the form of bank liquidity requirements and bank leverage ratios.

Nevertheless, the big banks remain implicitly insured by taxpayers and can consequently raise funds more cheaply than less strategically important banks that are deemed not to be too big or too complex to be allowed to fail. This gives the big banks a competitive advantage and reinforces their dominance. In response to this, systemically important financial institutions are increasingly required to hold supplementary capital as recommended by the Financial Stability Board (FSB, 2011), and attention is now turning to TLAC, the total loss absorbing capacity of banks and the banking system (Mullineux, 2014).

The GFC revealed problems with the regulatory approach to addressing externalities arising from excessive bank risk taking and from the 'too big (or complex) to fail' problem. A structural proposal to help solve the problem is to separate the investment and commercial banking activities of 'universal banks' within bank holding companies (BHCs) and to require them to operate as separately capitalized subsidiaries; with the aim of making it easier to let parts of the BHC fail while 'resolving' problems in the 'utility', or infrastructural, part of the bank, so that it can keep functioning without unduly disrupting payments systems and economic activity.

In the UK's Financial Services (Banking Reform) Act (2013), the 'ring fencing' of retail banking and some commercial banking, and thus the household and small business deposits, in line with the Independent Commission on Banking (ICB, 2011) and the Parliamentary Commission on Banking Standards (PCBS, 2013a) recommendations, was required to be implemented. Further, the UK's Prudential Regulatory Authority is to consider whether a US Volcker Rule (SEC, 2013), which limits the scope of the 'proprietary' trading and hedge fund business a bank can undertake with the aim of restricting the risk to which bank deposits can be exposed, is appropriate for 'The City' in London. Meanwhile, the EU is still considering the Liikanen Report proposals (Liikanen Group, 2012) for a more limited separation of retail and investment banking than is now required in the UK. A less strict separation seems likely given the long tradition of universal banking in Germany and elsewhere in continental Europe.

The debate about the pros and cons of universal banking is ongoing. Calomiris (2013) argues strongly that there are significant economies of scale and scope in banking and also major benefits from the cross-border operation and competition of universal banks, while acknowledging that size matters and robust *internationally agreed* resolution regimes need to be implemented as a back-stop.

Nonetheless, we consider regulatory reforms to be moving in the right direction. Keeping in mind the usefulness of regulations to ensure financial stability, we argue that the aforementioned regulatory and structural measures should be augmented by (fiscal) taxation and also that a fair balance between regulation and fiscal taxation should be aspired to. We propose that Adam Smith's (1776) widely accepted 'principles' of fairness and efficiency in taxation should be used to balance the regulatory and fiscal taxation of banks (and other financial institutions), noting that regulatory and fiscal taxes may potentially be interchangeable. The ultimate aim should be to tax banking activities, not just banks as variously defined in different countries and regionally regulated blocs, so as to include 'shadow banking' as well as mainstream banking.

In this report, we study how banks are regulated and taxed in a number of countries and analyse how they could be taxed to achieve a fair and efficient balance between regulatory and fiscal taxes. Additionally, we provide an overview of the taxation: of financial instrument trading (the Financial Transaction Tax, or FTT); of financial activities (the Financial Activities Tax, or FAT); and banking products and services using a Value Added Tax (VAT) or GST (Goods and Services Tax), as it is called in Australia and New Zealand.

We note that revenue from such taxes could be hypothecated in order to build 'bank resolution' and deposit guarantee funds, and also to finance bank supervisory authorities; which are normally funded out of general taxation or through levies on banks and other supervised financial institutions. Differential rates of taxation, like varying risk weights in the Basle risk-related capital adequacy requirements, might potentially be used to 'tax' risk taking at appropriate rates in order to promote financial stability and could be varied over time as a macro-prudential policy tool.

We support the elimination of the tax deductibility of the 'expensing' of interest on debt because current business tax rules encourage excessive debt issuance and favour debt over equity, which is in direct opposition to what bank regulations require, namely raising extra equity and reducing bank leverage to make banks safer. This in turn raises the question of whether tax deductibility of interest on debt should be removed from banks alone, as they are the licensed creators on credit.

We support the prevailing view that an FTT is economically inefficient because it reduces market trading volume and liquidity and increases volatility and the cost of capital for firms. This is especially the case if it is applied to the gross value at each stage of the settlement chain of a financial transaction – as initially proposed by the European Commission – unlike VAT; which is applicable at the end of the chain. The cumulative effect of charging each agent in a multi-step execution process can be substantial. An FTT may seem like a tax on banks and other financial institutions, but it is highly likely that a good proportion of the costs would be passed on to the end investors. A narrower and relatively low tax, such as the UK 'stamp duty' on equity sales (and house sales), is likely to be much less distortionary and now seems more likely to be adopted by the EU, or the Eurozone alone. It would however raise less revenue. But imposing an FTT on government bond sales would both raise the cost of government funding and be detrimental to the 'repo market',[1] which underpins the interbank markets and thus liquidity in the banking system, and now forms the basis of central bank interest rate-setting operations.

The originally proposed EU FTT was applicable to other non-participating member countries and to third countries if they were counterparty to financial transaction trading in an FTT jurisdiction. Equity issuance is already relatively more costly than debt issuance due to the tax deductibility of interest, but not dividend payments, and UK-style stamp duty adds to the cost of selling equities. Nevertheless, we might support a suitably low stamp duty as a revenue raiser whose major benefit might be to serve as a 'Tobin Tax' (Tobin, 1978) discouraging wasteful over-trading of shares and 'short termism' by throwing 'sand in the wheels' of the stock market.

We further propose the removal of the exemption of financial services from VAT in order to achieve greater efficiency in taxation, as recommended in the Mirrlees Review (Mirrlees et al., 2010) for the UK and the Henry Report (Henry, 2010) for Australia. It would also discourage over-use of financial services and the elimination of the distortionary UK 'free banking' system, based on cross-subsidization, and promote efficiency in the payments system (Mullineux, 2012). Given the operational difficulties linked to the removal of exemption from VAT, the cash flow method with Tax Collection Account proposed by Poddar and English (1997) is recommended.

We note the overlap between the UK Bank Levy (HM Treasury, 2010), which was initially designed to discourage reliance on wholesale money market funding in favour of retail deposits taking, but has increasingly been used to hit revenue-raising targets, and the proposed Basel III Liquidity Coverage Ratio (LCR). This should be rectified to eliminate double taxation. The best use of a bank levy, as proposed in the Eurozone, is to fund the build-up of a bank resolution and deposit insurance fund. Once the fund reaches a sufficient size, the levy should be phased out and replaced by a risk-related deposit insurance premium, as in the US, leaving banks' profits in the UK to be taxed in line with other companies once it is deemed that they have made a 'true and fair contribution' to the fiscal consolidation made necessary by the banking crisis and the major recession it precipitated.

Finally, we conclude that the proposed EU FTT is likely to reduce market liquidity while the proposed Basel III liquidity ratios (LCR and the Net Stable Funding Ratio) may also reduce money market liquidity because they require banks to hold more liquidity assets on their balance sheets. This may reduce the number of buyers in the market and could cause difficulties when many banks are seeking to sell liquid assets following a major adverse event. As with deposit insurance, the principle of pooling risks should underpin liquidity insurance, and so ever larger liquidity reserves within banks should be mitigated by a redefinition of a modern fit-for-purpose lender-of-last-resort liquidity support regime operated by central banks. As with deposit insurance, the implicit premium implied by conditions of access to the facilities should be risk related, in line with the Bagehot (1873) principles that have been relaxed since the onset of the GFC and further undermined in the face of the Eurozone crisis. In other words, deposit insurance premiums and conditions for access to central bank liquidity insurance should 'tax' risk taking.

The remainder of this Arts and Humanities Research Council 'FinCris' project report for its 'Taxing Banks Fairly' workstream is organized as follows: Chapter 2 draws a comparison between bank regulation and taxation; Chapter 3 reviews the causes of the GFC; Chapter 4 describes the fiscal costs of the GFC; Chapter 5 provides an overview of existing taxation and related issues; Chapter 6 discusses the taxation of financial instruments; and Chapter 7 provides a conclusion and policy recommendations.

Note

1. A repurchase agreement, or repo for short, is a type of short-term loan much used in the money markets, whereby the seller of a security agrees to buy it back at a specified price and time. The seller pays an interest

rate, called the repo rate, when buying back the securities (source: http://lexicon.ft.com/Term?term= repurchase-agreement (accessed 27 March 2015)).

2. Regulations and taxation

The International Monetary Fund (IMF, 2010) proposes the use of taxes and regulations to counteract micro- and macro-prudential risk in the financial system. Although regulations have traditionally been used to try to ensure banking stability, their focus has primarily been on micro-prudential regulation and supervision. The GFC emphasized the need for a macro-prudential framework that can address systemic risks and hence focus on the stability of the financial system as a whole. We portray the taxation of banks as a macro-prudential regulation. This idea of using regulatory 'taxes' and other micro- and macro-prudential policy measures, including the implementation of fiscal taxes and surcharges and credit controls, has been pursued by policy makers around the world for some time. For instance, a number of Asian countries, including Hong Kong, have long used restrictions on loan-to-value ratios, capital inflows and other ad hoc measures to limit internal or external vulnerabilities. Over a decade ago, the General Manager of the Bank for International Settlements (BIS), Andrew Crockett (2000), proposed marrying the bank-specific micro-prudential and the systemic macro-prudential dimensions of financial stability in a speech that proved prescient.

Keen (2011) considers the choice between taxation and regulation measures to bring about the stability of a financial system. He lists the following factors that can help balance tax and regulatory measures: 1) income effects; 2) uncertainty; 3) asymmetric information; and 4) institutional issues.

First, taxation strengthens public buffers to address bank failure and crisis, whereas regulation focuses on private buffers. For strongly correlated negative shocks, public buffers provide a useful risk-pooling role and reduce the incidence of bank failures. However, for strongly positively correlated shocks across institutions, the benefit of risk pooling and economy of scale disappears. Taxation is more beneficial in dealing with macro-prudential risks, whereas regulation, while leaving institutions to respond appropriately to systemic crises, may enable a more robust response to macro-prudential concerns.

Secondly, the comparison between taxation and regulation depends on the shape of private marginal cost and marginal external benefit (MEB), as demonstrated by Weitzman (1974). If the externalities are small, taxation will dominate (the MEB curve then being horizontal, at zero). However, in the case of a major bank failure, regulation is preferred because the external cost of failure exceeds the private benefits.

Thirdly, there is information asymmetry between the policy makers and the management of financial institutions with regard to the riskiness of their financial affairs, as well as the quality of their management. Banks differ in their ability to manage risk and to set up an optimal policy. In this case, a minimum capital requirement is useful to limit the risk-taking ability of banks. However, a nonlinear tax, with an increasing marginal rate on bank borrowing, can still be helpful.

Finally, as far as regulations are concerned, there have been some coordinated efforts towards the implementation of regulations at the global level; for example, Basel III. However, there has been little global effort to coordinate the enforcement of taxation. Nevertheless, there have been unilateral taxation innovations in different parts of the world. Recently, the European Parliament has taken an initiative to ask banks to report a breakdown of the taxes they pay in different jurisdictions; it is expected that the same practice will be implemented worldwide.

De Nicolò et al. (2012) study the impact of bank regulation and taxation in a dynamic setting, in which banks are exposed to capital and liquidity risk. They find that capital requirements can mitigate banks' incentives to take on the excessive risk induced by deposit insurance and limited liability, and can increase efficiency and welfare. By contrast, liquidity requirements significantly reduce lending, efficiency and welfare.

If these requirements are too strict, then the benefits of regulation disappear, and the associated efficiency and social costs may be significant. On taxation, corporate income taxes generate higher government revenues and entail lower efficiency and welfare costs than taxes on non-deposit liabilities. Coulter et al. (2013) argue that taxation and regulation are fundamentally the same; however, if taxes are paid ex ante, unless they are pure capital, the double-edged aspect of taxation arises.

The prevailing Basel II regulations were not able to prevent banks from taking excessive risks, forcing governments either to let them fail or bail them out in the GFC. Basel II consisted of three pillars: a minimum risk-weighted capital requirement, a supervisory review and market discipline. The calculation of credit risk exposures relied on assessment of risk-weighted assets. The idea is that because some assets are riskier than others, banks should hold more capital against riskier assets. There are two major problems attached to this: the calculation of risk weights was backward looking and thus assumed that the relative riskiness of assets would not change over time. In addition, it was assumed that sovereign bonds were riskless; regardless of which developed country issued them. Because Greece was part of the European Union, the bonds issued by the Greek Government carried the same zero weight as those issued by their German counterpart. The problem with this approach became evident with the onset of the Eurozone crisis in 2010, after which Greek government bonds carried a higher risk premium in the bond markets than German 'bunds'.

Further, banks with similar portfolios can potentially use quite different risk weights in their modelling of portfolio risks. The supervisors allow big banks with large trading books to use their own internal models to determine the riskiness of their asset portfolios and to hold capital based on their own risk assessments. On the other hand, there are explicit risk-weighted capital requirements for traditional loans. Consequently, bigger banks with large trading books can hold proportionately less capital and still report higher capital ratios, compared with smaller banks whose portfolios contain mostly traditional loans.

Furthermore, the preferred approach for the calculation of market risk was value-at-risk (VaR).[1] Taleb (2010) famously highlighted the ignorance of underestimation of the risks in the falsely assumed normal distribution tails. Nocera (2009) argues that the whole VaR structure gives banks an incentive to push risk into the 'tails' of the statistical distribution, which essentially 'fattens' them and significantly increases banking risk. Therefore, it is important that we can estimate the 'tail-risks' of banks.

Basel III (BIS, 2011) requires banks to increase their capital ratios in order to make them more resilient. This helps to address the moral hazard problem created by implicit taxpayer insurance of banks and also helps to reassure depositors. Furthermore, as highlighted by Mullineux (2012), the increased emphasis on core equity will put the small mutual saving banks at a disadvantage because they cannot issue equity, potentially reducing diversity in banking: which is widely seen as beneficial (Mullineux, 2014).

An issue highlighted by the Parliamentary Commission on Banking Standards report (PCBS, 2013a) is that the proposed Basel III capital leverage ratio[2] of 3 percent is too low, and that it should be substantially higher than this level.[3] Admati and Hellwig (2013) favour an equity ratio of 30 per cent or more and argue that it will not reduce the lending capacity of banks; rather, it will increase it because banks will become less risky and able to raise equity more cheaply from the capital market. Because the leverage ratio is implemented on a gross and non-weighted basis, it might encourage banks to increase their exposure to high-risk, high-return lending and could potentially increase their risk exposures and lending to small and medium-sized enterprises (SMEs), *inter alia*, helping to overcome the credit crunch perhaps. The parallel Basel risk-weighted capital adequacy requirements would limit this tendency, however, and the balance between the leverage and risk-weighted capital ratios needs to be carefully thought through to avoid double taxation and distortions.

The issue of whether increased capital (and liquidity) ratios will impede lending, especially to the largely bank-dependent SMEs (Bernanke and Gertler, 1995) is of major political and economic importance. Modigliani and Miller (1958) suggest it should not matter in what proportions banks use debt and equity funding, provided there are no tax distortions, *inter alia*. But, clearly the tax system contains a bias towards debt finance that needs to be addressed. One option is to remove tax deductibility of interest for all firms, or perhaps just banks; and certainly not SMEs given that they remain largely bank dependent, although with 'crowdfunding' and 'invoice discounting' via the internet increasingly available the dependency may decline over time. Another is to create equivalent deductibility with regard to dividend payments, and thereby remove the often alleged 'double taxation' of saving. Admati and Hellwig (2013), with support from the IMF (Klein, 2014), go further in arguing that well-capitalized (and regulated and supervised) banks may actually lend more to SMEs and in general, and will be better able to manage their risks.

In considering the balance between regulatory and fiscal taxes, the principle of 'risk pooling' in insurance (Bodie et al., 2013) should be borne in mind. Capital (and liquidity) requirements are imposed on individual banks and can be regarded as in-house insurance funds. It is generally cheaper and more efficient for those seeking to insure to pay into a pooled fund, rather than hold sizeable precautionary reserves against risks such as houses burning down or car accidents or theft. Pooling reduces the average risk and is thus cheaper.

Thus if the banks pay into deposit insurance and bank resolution funds, they need hold less in-house insurance. Further, the central bank, as 'lender of last resort', can decide on the extent and at what cost it provides liquidity insurance to the banks, and thus the size of the liquidity reserves they need hold. As long as the insurance premiums are appropriately risk related, there should be no moral hazard issues. The risk weights upon which the premiums would be based are related to those used in calculating risk-related capital adequacy under the Basel III framework. To minimize distortions and unintended consequences, the trick is to get the risk weights, and thus the risk premiums, right. The resolution and deposit insurance funds can be raised via risk-related levies on individual banks – which is probably least distortionary and directly taxes riskiness – or out of financial sector taxes, as proposed with the Eurozone-wide bank levy (EC, 2010). Financial stability can be regarded as a 'Public Good' (Samuelson, 1954) and so taxpayers may indeed be expected to contribute to the cost of its provision and must decide how much of it they want. To be perfectly safe, 'banks' would have to eschew credit risk exposures and cease lending, but if bank lending contributes significantly to growth, then we want banks to take risks, but to manage them appropriately, so that implicit taxpayer insurance is reduced. But how far should it in fact be reduced? This is a public policy issue (Mullineux, 2013, 2014). Further, 'taxing' banks risks pushing some parts of banking into the 'shadows' to avoid regulatory and pecuniary taxation and requires extending appropriate regulation and taxation – including consideration of relative corporate, income and Capital Gains Tax levels – to the 'shadow banking' sector, as proposed by the FSB in October 2014 (FSB, 2014).

While micro-prudential supervision focuses on individual institutions, macro-prudential supervision aims to mitigate risks to the financial system as a whole ('systemic risks'). The Bank of England (2009) highlighted that macro-prudential policy was missing in the prevailing policy framework and the gap between macro-prudential policy and micro-prudential supervision had widened over the previous decade. After the advent of the 2007 financial crisis, improved measures have been devised to measure the macro-economic impact of the financial institutions. These include: conditional value-at-risk, by Adrian and Brunnermeier (2011); Systemic Expected Shortfall, by Acharya et al. (2010), proposing a tax on the default risk of a bank; and the Market-based tax by Hart and Zingales (2009), proposing a bank tax on the value of credit default swap contracts.

Macro-prudential supervision primarily focuses on reducing asset price inflation and preventing 'bubbles', and thus the need to insure against bank failure when asset price 'bubbles' burst. Hence it protects taxpayers from the need for bail-outs. The proposed tools include 'mortgage or home loan the (house price) to value' and 'loan to income' ratios; which can be raised in response to increasing asset price inflation. They are essentially credit controls that can be regarded as a targeted 'tax' on mortgage lending.

Additional macro-prudential tools have been proposed to counter the pro-cyclicality of the banking system caused by risk-related capital adequacy, 'mark to market' accounting and backward-looking provisioning against bad and doubtful debts. Examples of these are counter-cyclical capital and liquidity requirements and non-risk-related capital ('leverage') ratios; a levy on the outstanding debt multiplied with a factor of average time-to-maturity of a bank; a levy on non-core liabilities (Perotti and Suarez, 2009; Hanson et al., 2011; Shin, 2011); and forward-looking provisioning, for which allowance has been made via changes in the international accounting standards to permit forward-looking 'general' provisioning (Gaston and Song, 2014).

These macro-prudential instruments are largely untested as yet, although the US Federal

Deposit Insurance Fund collects risk-related insurance premiums from banks and serves as a resolution fund for banks that are not 'too big to fail', and the Hong Kong Monetary Authority had been setting loan-to-value ratios for home loans for some time (HKMA, 2013). There is a worry that it may prove politically difficult for public access to affordable mortgage finance to be limited through loan-to-value and loan-to-income ratios manipulated by an unelected Prudential Regulation Authority (PRA) at the Bank of England.

The Eurozone member countries reached an agreement on 18 December 2013 to form a 'Banking Union' which will have three pillars: a Single Supervisory Mechanism (SSM), a Single Resolution Mechanism (SRM) and a common deposit guarantee scheme (DGS). The SSM came into operation, coordinated and overseen by the European Central Bank (ECB) working with national central banks of the member countries, in November 2014 following a Comprehensive Assessment of the banks to be supervised. The assessment involved an Asset Quality Review undertaken by the ECB and Stress Tests of the banks by the European Banking Authority, the EU banking regulator. It is proposed that a common bank levy is used to build up, over a number of years, a Bank Recovery and Resolution Fund. The aim is to protect taxpayers from having to bail out banks. To achieve this, however, a very large, hopefully normally idle, fund would be required. In the US, the FDIC[4] is underwritten by the Treasury and cannot afford to resolve the problems of large banks. The FDIC, it should be noted, is funded using risk-related premiums levied on banks, and 'holidays' are granted when funds reach target levels in times when there are few calls on the funds.

The UK could possibly use its Bank Levy to establish a pre-funded resolution fund to make the recently enacted 'depositor preference', or debt seniority over all bond holders, a reality; but a deposit guarantee scheme funded using risk-related premiums paid by banks, in line with the US, might be better. The trouble is that most of UK banking is done by a few large banks that could not be bailed out using the fund. For a UK deposit insurance corporation to work along US lines, the big banks would have to be broken up.

The UK Financial Services (Banking Reform) Act and EU Banking Union agreement both establish depositor preference, with the Eurozone providing for the 'bailing-in' of junior and senior bond holders in accordance with credit standings. This means that the bond holders have to share losses in accordance with their credit seniority, once shareholders have taken their losses, before government assistance to rescue banks is provided.

Alongside all this re-regulation, broader interest in financial sector taxation has been increasing. The European Commission's report on financial sector taxation (EC, 2010) puts forward three arguments in favour of the use of taxation. First, taxation, in addition to regulations, is considered to be a corrective measure to reduce the risk-taking activities by the financial sector. Secondly, it is a source of revenue through which banks, underpinned by taxpayers, can make a 'fair contribution' to public finances. Thirdly, it is a source of funding for the resolution of failed banks. The UK Bank Levy is perhaps best regarded as making a fair contribution to compensate taxpayers for the fiscal consolidation, or 'austerity', made necessary by the need to bail them out and mount a fiscal stimulus to head off a full-blown economic recession following the GFC. The use of taxes alongside regulations to reduce risk-taking activity requires them to be carefully balanced in order to avoid double taxation, as we have noted.

Other studies, such as those of Shaviro (2011) and Ceriani et al. (2011) have, however, argued that taxes have the potential to exacerbate behaviours that may have contributed to the crisis. For instance, tax rules encouraging excessive debt, as we have noted, complex financial transactions, poorly designed incentive compensation for corporate managers and highly leveraged home-ownership may all have contributed to the crisis. The last observation has been strongly supported by a recent book by Mian and Sufi (2014), who present a strong case that the US subprime crisis was caused by over-indebtedness, and the subsequent household deleveraging was the major cause of the 'Great American Recession' that followed. The prevention of a future cycle of housing debt requires replacing debt-based contracts with equity-based home purchase contracts that allow risk sharing and provide for more debt forgiveness. Because firms can deduct interest expenses from their payable taxes, this gives a tax advantage to debt finance. Tax deductibility of interest on home loans is still permitted in the US, where there are also implicit subsidies through mortgage loan guarantees by government-sponsored agencies. Switzerland and a number of other countries also allow tax deductibility of interest on mortgages, but they were removed in the UK over a decade ago. 'Debt bias' is recognized in the wider public finance literature (Auerbach and Gordon, 2002). Bank lending by borrowing short, increasingly in the wholesale money markets, to make long-term home loans, and thus engaging in positive asset transformation, which exposed banks to increasing liquidity risk, increasing their leverage, clearly increased financial fragility; but in order to lend, there must be willing borrowers (Mian and Sufi, 2014).

Ceriani et al. (2011) consider the taxation of residential buildings and the deductibility of mortgage interest, the taxation of stock options and other performance-based remuneration, and the interaction between securitization and the tax system. They argue that these three kinds of taxation contributed to the GFC and that the repeal of capital gains taxation on home selling through the 1997 US Tax Relief Act was particularly important.

In the US there is evidence of preferential tax treatment on the employer's side, which may have contributed to the success of stock-based remuneration plans. Stock options, however, encourage managers to aim for short-term profits instead of having a long-term focus. Furthermore, Ceriani et al. (2011) argue that securitization creates opportunities for tax arbitrage and reduces the total tax paid by the originator, the special purpose vehicle (SPV) and the final investor. Because of tax differences in different countries, the SPV may be a tax-free vehicle under foreign law. The SPV offsets incomes that are otherwise taxed at a different rate by pooling interest incomes, capital gains and losses. It also defers the tax until the SPV distributes incomes on the securities it has issued or profits are realized.

In the next chapter, we briefly review the, still debated, causes of the financial crisis in order to identify the regulatory issues at stake and the political motivation to increase the level and range of taxes on the financial sector.

Notes

1. VaR is a statistical model that gives the probability of certainty (X per cent) that more than a certain amount of dollars will not be lost in the next N days. For example, if we have $10 million of daily VaR with a 99 percent confidence interval, it means that we are 99 per cent confident that we will not lose more than $10 million today.
2. Note that there is a difference between leverage ratio and risk-weighted assets (RWA) capital ratios. Leverage ratio is the ratio of tier 1 capital to average total assets, whereas RWA tier 1 capital ratio is the tier 1 capital divided by the risk-weighted assets. RWA are the assets weighted according to their risk.
3. In October 2014 it was anticipated that the PRA at the Bank of England would set the rate at 5 percent, and thus above the Basel requirements.
4. Federal Deposit Insurance Corporation (FDIC): a US government agency that guarantees to a limited extent deposits at member institutions and also provides financial assistance to help achieve mergers and prevent failure (http://lexicon.ft.com/Term?term= Federal-Deposit-Insurance-Corporation (accessed 27 March 2015)).

3. Some lessons from the Global, or Great, Financial Crisis

In an environment of historically low interest rates, low returns and plentiful liquidity, investors actively sought higher yields; often through capital gains from rising asset prices. Risk was widely mispriced due to lax internal controls at banks and other financial institutions. As a result, an increased number of innovative and complex instruments were designed to offer more attractive yields, often combined with increased leverage. Specifically, financial institutions securitized their loans into mortgage-backed securities, which were subsequently converted into collateralized obligations (CDOs and CLOs), generating a dramatic expansion of leverage within the financial system as a whole.[1]

Financial institutions engaged in very high capital leverage ratios in pursuit of historically high returns on their equity; leaving them highly vulnerable to even a small decline in underlying asset (property) values, or even their rate of increase. The institutional shareholders came to expect banks to pursue high returns on equity, leading to large dividend pay-outs, and governments, particularly in the UK, where the financial sector was nearly four times GDP, were happy to reap the consequently substantial tax revenues form profits, high salaries and large bonuses. Meanwhile, the real wages of the middle- to low-income earners in the US had been stagnant for a number of years and so there was a 'growth imperative' and a need for easy access to credit to boost the consumption levels of this important set of voters (Rajan, 2011). Following the recession in the early 1990s, UK growth was also consumer debt fuelled and, ahead of the financial crisis, subprime mortgage lending was expanding; though not on the scale that it had in the US (Gibbons, 2014; Mian and Sufi, 2014).

Failures in risk assessment and management were further aggravated by the remuneration and incentive schemes within the financial institutions. These contributed to excessive risk taking by rewarding the short-term expansion of the volume of subprime mortgage lending and risky trades; rather than the long-term profitability of patient investment. Moreover, these pressures were not contained by regulatory or supervisory policy or practice and regulations were not effective in mitigating these risks. For example, capital requirements were particularly light on proprietary trading transactions, while the risks involved in these transactions proved to be much higher than the banks' internal models had predicted (EC, 2011).

Many governments realized that allowing major individual banks and other systemic financial institutions to fail might be detrimental to the national and global economy. But there was no simple way for 'systemically important' banks to continue to provide essential banking functions while in insolvency. Large banks could not simply be shut down without significant systemic damage. Although the actions that governments were forced to take in order to deal with banking institutions in distress (capital injections, guarantees and loans) managed to stabilize their financial systems, they also propped up failing institutions and supported shareholders, bond holders and depositors, at a huge potential cost to taxpayers.

Further, as noted above, the tax deductibility of interest has the potential to encourage the leveraging behaviour that contributed to the crisis (Ceriani et al., 2011; Shaviro, 2011).

Note

1. See De Larosière (2009), Hemmelgarn et al. (2011) and Hemmelgarn and Nicodeme (2010) for more detail.

4. Fiscal costs of the Global Financial Crisis

Many G20 countries provided significant support to their financial sectors during the GFC.[1] Although the magnitude and nature of support measures varied across countries, with support in advanced countries being preponderant, interventions were generally bold. These support measures included recapitalization and partial nationalization, asset purchases and swaps, asset/liability guarantees, extended deposit insurance, and liquidity support.

This chapter does not attempt to go further than identifying direct bail-out costs and does not take account of the fiscal stimuli required after the financial crisis to avert a depression, potentially on the scale of the Great Depression of the 1930s. These fiscal interventions were supported, in contrast to the 1930s, with massive monetary stimuli involving low interest rates and 'unconventional' 'Quantitative (and Qualitative) Easing' (QE), led by central banks; particularly in the US, the UK and then Japan and, latterly, the EU. Another depression was averted, but nevertheless there was a 'Great Recession'. The fiscal stimuli led to a rise in government debt, taking the place of falling private, particularly household, debt to avert the depression, but 'austere' fiscal consolidation was embarked upon by some countries; arguably too much too soon, resulting in a slow, drawn-out recovery. At the time of writing, 'normalization' of interest rates was being contemplated, but would interest rates be raised too far too soon?

Fiscal austerity clearly entails ongoing costs of the crisis, and the failure to resume pre-crisis rates of growth points to further losses of tax revenues. Also ignored here are other implicit subsidies to banks through cheap funding by central banks with relaxed collateral requirements, on the one hand, and growing 'financial repression' in an attempt to reduce the cost of servicing the significantly higher public debt.

Banks have been encouraged to hold more liquid reserves, often in the form of short-term government debt, and longer-term government bonds, as assets. Low and falling interest rates on this debt reduces government funding costs while providing banks with appreciating assets; as bond prices move inversely with their yields. The ending of QE and 'normalization' of interest rates and longer-term yields will unwind the 'repression' and increase the cost of servicing government debt and the cost to the banks of the higher, post-crisis 'Basel' liquidity requirements, further 'taxing' banks.

The focus here is more narrowly on the fiscal costs of supporting the banks following the Lehman Brothers collapse in September 2008. It should be noted that, to the extent that the bail-out involves the state, through a 'bad bank' or (impaired) 'asset management corporation' (AMC), buying impaired assets and bad loans from banks, and perhaps other financial institutions, some of the initial costs can be defrayed by auctioning the impaired loan at a discount or gaining control of the collateral (often real estate), holding the assets and then selling them into a recovering market after a period of time. The costs then relate to the discounts offered, the prices gained on sale of real estate and the opportunity cost of the capital tied up in the AMC. In the US, the central bank (the 'Fed') also bought mortgage-backed securities at a discount on the secondary market as part of its QE programme and has been able to sell them at a higher price as the real estate markets recovered, or benefit from holding them to maturity. It is still too early to gauge what the final 'fiscal' costs of supporting the banks will prove to be, but these must be set against the benefits of averting a widespread systemic financial crisis and a second great depression.

In this chapter, the estimated first-round fiscal costs are reviewed, followed by a brief stock-take of the ongoing estimates of the narrowly defined fiscal costs of the bail-out.

4.1 Initial financing requirements and pledged support

There was significant variation in the announced or pledged support for capital injections and purchase of assets across developed and emerging economies. By the end of December 2009, the advanced G20 economies had pledged $1220 billion of capital injections and $756 billion of asset purchases, equivalent to 3.8 and 2.4 per cent of GDP, respectively (Table 4.1). The corresponding amounts in the emerging G20 economies were $90 and $18 billion, respectively; 0.7 and 0.1 per cent of GDP (Table 4.1). In addition, Table 4.1 shows that within both groups, there was significant variation in the announced amounts allocated in these two categories, with the bulk in advanced economies accounted for by Germany, Japan, the UK and the US, while others provided no support. IMF (2010) shows that substantial funds were pledged to guarantee banks' wholesale debt and interbank liabilities, almost entirely in advanced economies (10.9 per cent of the GDP of advanced G20 economies, as shown in Table 4.1). Central bank support was provided primarily through the expansion of credit lines; scaling-up of liquidity provisions; purchases of asset-backed securities; widening of the list of assets eligible as collateral; and lengthening of the maturities of long-term refinancing operations (7.7 per cent of GDP of advanced G20 economies, as shown in Table 4.1). Several governments also expanded the coverage of deposit insurance to different types of deposits or raised the limits for the amounts covered so as to maintain depositor confidence. Moreover, these governments show that financing requirements largely reflected injection of capital and purchase of assets, with the upfront commitment of such support estimated at 5.0 and 0.2 per cent of GDP for the advanced and emerging G20 countries, respectively. Although guarantees, as well as central bank support and liquidity provisions, did not require upfront financing in most cases, they led to a significant build-up of contingent liabilities.

4.2 Utilization of the support to the financial sector

An IMF survey (IMF, 2010) finds that the utilized amounts of financial sector support have been much lower than the pledged amounts. Table 4.2 indicates that for advanced G20 economies, the average amount utilized for capital injection was 2.1 per cent of GDP, that is, $653 billion, or just over half the pledged amount. The figures in Table 4.2 indicate that France, Germany, the US and the UK accounted for over 90 per cent of this. For the advanced economies, the utilized amount for asset purchases was around 1.4 per cent of GDP, less than two-thirds of the pledged amount, while the uptake of guarantees has been

Table 4.1   Amount announced or pledged for financial sector services, by country (in percentage of 2009 GDP unless otherwise stated)

Country	Capital Injection	Purchase of Assets and Lending by Treasury*	Direct Support**	Guarantees***	Asset Swap and Purchase of Financial Assets, including Treasuries, by Central Bank	Upfront Government Financing****
	(A)	(B)	(A+B)	(C)	(D)	(E)
Advanced Economies						
Australia	0	0	0	13.2	0	0
Canada	0	9.1	9.1	0	0	9.1
France	1.3	0.2	1.5	16.9	0	1.1
Germany	3.4	0	3.4	17.2	0	3.4
Italy	1.3	0	1.3	0	2.7	2.7
Japan	2.5	4.1	6.6	7.2	0	0.4
Korea	1.2	1.5	2.7	11.6	0	0.8
United Kingdom	8.2	3.7	11.9	40	28.2	8.7
United States	5.1	2.3	7.4	7.5	12.1	7.4

Emerging Economies						
Brazil	0	0.8	0.8	0.5	0	0
Russia	7.1	0.5	7.7	0	0	1.9
G20 Average	**2.6**	**1.4**	**4**	**6.4**	**4.6**	**3.1**
Advanced Economies	3.8	2.4	6.2	10.9	7.7	5
In billions of US$	1,220	756	1,976	3,530	2,400	1,610
Emerging Economies	0.7	0.1	0.8	0	0	0.2
In billions of US$	90	18	108	7	0	24

Notes: * excludes Treasury funds provided in support of central bank operations.

**includes some elements that do not require upfront government financing.

*** excludes deposit insurance provided by deposit insurance agencies.

**** includes gross support measures that require upfront government outlays. Excludes recovery from the sale of acquired assets.

Sources: (1) The figures in the table are IMF staff estimates based on the G20 survey where columns A, B, C, D and E indicate announced or pledged amounts, and not actual uptake. (2) The table is adapted from IMF (2010).

Table 4.2 Financial sector support utilized relative to announcement, by country (in percentage of 2009 GDP unless otherwise stated)

	Capital Injection		Purchase of Assets and Lending by Treasury	
	Amount Used	In Percentage of Announcement	Amount Used	In Percentage of Announcement
Advanced Economies				
Canada	0	–	4.4	48.4
France	1.1	83.2	0	0
Germany	1.2	35	3.7	–
Italy	0.3	20.3	0	–
Japan	0.1	2.4	0.1	1.4
Korea	0.4	32.5	0.1	3.8
United Kingdom	6.4	78.5	0.1	4
United States	2.9	57	1.9	84
Emerging Economies				
Brazil	0	–	0.3	43.5
Russia	3.1	43	0	0

G20 Average	1.3	51.7	0.9	60.2
Advanced Economies	2	52.3	1.4	61
In billions of US$	639	–	461	–
Emerging Economies	0.3	43	0.03	27.5
In billion of US$	38.4	–	5	–

Sources: The figures in this table are from the IMF staff estimates based on the G20 survey. The table is adapted from IMF (2010).

markedly lower than pledged. The amounts utilized in the G20 emerging market countries have been proportionately lower.

The IMF (2010) report identified several reasons for the generally low amounts utilized. First, they reflect the precautionary nature of initial pledges as a result of the uncertainties prevailing at the time and the need to err on the side of caution so as to increase market confidence. Secondly, they reflect more efficient use of government resources, such as using capital injections rather than asset purchases. Thirdly, they reflect the increasing stability of market conditions and improving bank liquidity following significant 'lender of last resort' intervention by central banks to pump liquidity into banking systems. Lastly, lags in implementation of programmes for recapitalization and purchase of assets may have played a role, as has perhaps been the case in the Eurozone.

4.3   Net cost of support measures (instruments) and recovery of assets

The IMF (2010) report notes that many of the support arrangements were structured in such a fashion that the financial sector would pay, at least in part, for the cost of the support over time. For instance, recoveries related to the capitalization efforts would reflect repurchases, dividends and the sale of warrants. Banks paid to participate in asset protection schemes, and were charged sign-up and exit fees. Fees were also received for the provision of guarantees by governments, as in the UK. To boost the deposit insurance funds, monies were sometimes recouped from special levies imposed on the banking sector.

Once the financial markets had stabilized post-March 2009, some recovery of asset prices began.[2] Figures from the survey responses presented in Table 4.3 suggest that, for advanced G20 economies, recovery was sustained largely through repurchases of shares, fees and interest income, and to a very small extent, the sale of assets. Taking into account these data, the net direct cost of recapitalization and asset purchases was estimated to average 2.8 per cent of GDP, equivalent to $877 billion, and 1.8 per cent of GDP for the G20 as a whole. Guarantee measures were used more extensively than in previous crises, while total expenditures in public recapitalization to address the crisis were slightly below historical norms.

The direct net budgetary cost appears to be below historical norms, reflecting extensive use of containment measures, such as widespread central bank intervention utilizing unconventional monetary policy (asset purchases and easy lending to banks) in order to hold interest rates close to the zero lower bound, which reduced the actual cost and boosted asset prices, aiding recovery rates on sales of impaired assets and assets pledged in return for support. Historically,

*Table 4.3   Recovery of outlays and net direct cost of
financial sector support (in percentage of
2009 GDP unless otherwise stated)*

	Direct Support		Recovery	Net Direct Cost
	Pledged	Utilized		
G20 Average	**4**	**2.2**	**0.4**	**1.8**
Advanced Economies	6.2	3.5	0.8	2.8
In billions of US$	1,976	1,114	237	877
Emerging Economies	0.8	0.3	–	0.3
In billions of US$	108	43	–	43

Source: The figures in the table are from the IMF staff
estimates based on the G20 survey (IMF, 2010).

the net cost of guarantees has tended to be much
lower than that of capital injections or asset
purchases. Moreover, the IMF (2010) report
argues that general fiscal support to the economy
through 'automatic stabilizers' and discretionary
fiscal stimuli helped stabilize the financial sector
and improve the prospects for recovery by limiting the negative feedback loops between the
financial sector and the real economy.

Historically, countries have had to engage in
'fiscal consolidation', or deficit reduction, post-
crisis and this is the phase that the US and many
European countries, including the UK, entered
from 2010. The speed of reduction and degree of

'austerity' required is a market-conditioned political choice, but there is a trade-off between the
speed and nature of the fiscal retrenchment (mix
of government expenditure cuts and tax
increases) and current and future economic
growth prospects.

The IMF (2010) report states that for those G20
countries that experienced systemic financial crisis, the costs are comparable to earlier episodes.
In fact, the broader measures of costs, in terms of
the fiscal impact of induced recessions and real
economic costs, are estimated to be broadly similar to past crisis episodes. For instance, Laeven
and Valencia (2010) show the average increase in
public debt to be about 24 per cent of GDP and
the output losses to be about 26 per cent of
potential GDP for those countries which experienced a systemic banking crisis in 2007–2009.
They note that these estimates are not significantly different from historical averages, and
argue that this time around policies to address
potential banking insolvency were implemented
much more promptly than in the past; which
may have contributed to keeping direct outlays
relatively low.

The IMF (2010) report also notes that total debt
burdens had risen dramatically for almost all
G20 countries as a result of the crisis and, in
addition, uncertainty in the markets persisted, in
part relating to the high-risk exposures of sovereign balance sheets.

4.4   A stock-take of fiscal costs of the bail-out five years on

Five years on, the cost of the US bail-out of the financial sector has been recovered with a positive interest contribution to defraying the opportunity cost of investing the capital used in the Troubled Asset Relief (TARP) programme. The full cost of QE, which may ultimately result in Fed balance sheet losses and has been distortionary, has not been taken into the reckoning. Some estimations have been made that the GFC cost the US economy $6 trillion to $14 trillion and could possibly be twice that much if the untold implicit cost to 'too big to fail' institutions were included (Luttrell et al., 2013).

However, apart from the Netherlands, no other EU country could recover more than half of the cost of bail-out (see Table 4.4). This is perhaps evidence that the US economy has completely recovered from the GFC, but not in terms of the GDP lost because of the GFC. It is argued that the total US GDP would have been much more than current levels, had there been no crisis. Note also that, in terms of per cent of GDP, the cost of bail-out in the US is the smallest as compared with the EU countries, showing the size of the financial sector is much smaller in terms of GDP compared with the EU countries. The financial sectors of some of the small peripheral EU countries like Slovenia and Cyprus are really in a bad shape as they have not been successful in paying back any money (IMF, 2014a, 2014b, 2014c).

Table 4.4   Financial sector support (in percentage of 2013 GDP)

	Impact on Gross Public Debt and Other Support	Recovery, Per cent of total
Belgium	7.5	42.7
Cyprus	10.9	–
Denmark	6.0	41.7
Germany	12.5	15.2
Greece	30.9	22.0
Ireland	40.1	17.2
Netherlands	18.7	75.9
Portugal	10.7	0.7
Slovenia	12	–
Spain	7.7	40.3
United Kingdom	10.3	20.4
United States	4.5	106.7
Average	7.4	58.1

Sources: The figures in the table are from the IMF Fiscal Monitor (IMF, 2014b) and from the Eurostat Database.

Notes

1. Information in this chapter is based on that provided in Appendix 1 of the IMF (2010) report, which is based on responses to survey questionnaires sent to all G20 members in early December 2009. In the questionnaire, countries were requested to review and update staff estimates of direct support to financial sectors, consisting of recapitalization and asset purchases; liquidity

support comprising asset swaps and treasury purchases; and contingent support consisting of deposit
insurance and guarantees. The period covered by the
survey was June 2007 to December 2009.

2. The IMF (2010) report states that for cross-country
consistency, 'recovery' here does not include unreal-
ized gains on assets acquired by the public sector as
part of the financial sector support package, but occurs
only when these gains are realized as the assets are
divested.

5. An overview of existing taxation

We next give a comprehensive overview of the existing tax regimes applied to the financial sector. Following EC (2011), we consider three areas of taxation: corporate income tax; specific anti-avoidance rules or debt bias; and labour taxation.

5.1 Corporate income tax

There are two main differences between financial and non-financial corporations. This concerns the treatment of bad and doubtful loans and the non-application of thin capitalization rules to the financial sector. As far as bad and doubtful loans are concerned, the differential treatment may provide a cash-flow (liquidity) advantage, but not a tax advantage. These differences in treatment can be attributed to the structure of the business in the financial sector for which interest received and paid constitute part of the banking business and not just the financing of activities. Before the GFC, the financial sector accounted for a substantial share of corporate tax receipts. The values for the EU27 are similar to those for many non-EU G20 countries: about one-quarter in Canada, Italy and Turkey, and about a fifth in Australia, France, the UK and US (see Table 5.1 for detail).

Table 5.1   G20 corporate taxes paid by the financial sector (in per cent)

	Period	Share of Corporate Taxes	Share of Total Tax Revenue
Argentina	2006–2008	6	1
Australia	FY 2007	15	2.8
Brazil	2006–2008	15.4	1.8
Canada	2006–2007	23.5	2.6
France	2006–2008	18	1.9
Italy	2006–2008	26.3	1.7
Mexico	2006–2008	11.2	3.1
South Africa	FY 2007–2008	13.7	3.5
South Korea	2006–2008	17.7	3
Turkey	2006–2008	23.6	2.1
United Kingdom	FY 2006–2008	20.9	1.9
United States	FY 2006–2007	18.2	1.9
Unweighted Average		17.5	2.3

Source: The figures in this table are based on the IMF staff estimates based on G20 survey.

5.2   Specific anti-avoidance rules or debt bias

In order to reduce the tax due, companies utilize the applicable tax regime to their advantage. For example, they can choose to be funded via equity or debt. Debt financing generally brings additional tax benefits, compared with equity financing, because interest expenses are generally tax deductible (whereas dividends are distributed after tax and are not deductible).

The IMF (2010) argues that a preference for debt financing could in principle be offset by taxes at a personal level. Relatively light taxation of capital gains favours equity, for instance. However, in reality, the importance of tax-exempt and non-resident investors, the prevalence of avoidance schemes focused on creating interest deductions and the common discourse of market participants suggest that debt is often strongly tax favoured. In fact, Weichenrieder and Klautke (2008) show that debt bias leads to noticeably higher leverage for non-financial companies. Moreover, the proliferation prior to the crisis of hybrid instruments, such as Trust Preferred Securities (Engel et al., 1999), attracting interest in deduction yet allowable (subject to limits) as regulatory capital, strongly suggests tax incentives are conflicting with regulatory objectives.

With the objective of discouraging excessive or abusive use of financing methods that impact the tax base, the majority of countries have introduced anti-avoidance rules, which may be general or specific.[1]

5.2.1 Thin capitalization rules

To limit risk in the case of excessive debt financing, which creates solvency risk for creditors, and so minimize the adverse tax consequences of excessive interest 'expensing', several countries have set up 'thin capitalization rules', or rules limiting interest deductibility. These rules deny interest deduction once debt ratios or interest payment exceed some threshold. In other words, thin capitalization rules determine how much of the interest paid on corporate debt is deductible for tax purposes, thus limiting the amount of interest deducted when a certain debt-to-equity ratio is exceeded. In certain countries, including the Netherlands, rules also provide for a limitation of interest expenses, for instance when they exceed interest income. Countries where thin capitalization rules apply may be divided into two groups: Austria, Germany, Lithuania, the Netherlands, Poland, Portugal and the USA, in which thin capitalization rules apply in the same way to the banking sector as they do to other sectors; and the Czech Republic, Hungary, Switzerland, the UK and China, in which the thin capitalization rules apply to banks, but in a different way. The difference could be for various reasons. For instance, it may be in the applicable debt-to-equity ratio. For example, in China and the Czech Republic, the debt-to-equity ratio applicable to banks is higher. Alternatively, the difference may also be present in the borrowings, which have to be taken into account to compute the debt-to-equity ratio. For instance, in Hungary, banks do not take into account their liabilities in connection with their financial services activities, and in the UK, a group's external borrowings are not taken into account to determine the debt cap restriction.

A third group includes: Bulgaria, Denmark, France, Greece, Latvia, Romania, Slovenia and Spain, in which banks are excluded from the thin capitalization rules.

In Germany, thin capitalization rules are similar for banks and companies in other sectors. In practice, however, due to the fact that interest expenses are always deductible to the extent they do not exceed interest income earned, banks will not be burdened by the thin capitalization rules in this country. Table 5.2 provides an overview of Thin Capitalization Rules in different countries.

5.2.2 *A Comprehensive Business Income Tax*

The IMF (2010) proposes a Comprehensive Business Income Tax (CBIT), which would deny interest deductibility for Corporate Income Tax (CIT) altogether. Similarly, it would exempt interest received, in order to avoid multiple taxation within the corporate sector. Although CBIT would also result in financial institutions paying little or no CIT by virtue of having no tax due on interest received, but non-interest deductible costs, in aggregate this might be more than offset

Table 5.2 Overview of thin capitalization rules

Country	1. Do you have thin capitalization rules in your country?	2. Are these thin capitalization rules applicable to related-party interest?	3. Are these thin capitalization rules applicable to third-party interest?	4. Do thin capitalization rules apply to banks?	If your answer to question 4 is yes, please specify, if applicable, the difference between the thin capitalization rules for banks and the thin capitalization rules for companies of other sectors / non-banks
Austria	Yes	Yes	No	Yes	A specific minimum equity is required for banks (according to Basel II). Generally, for branches of foreign banks endowment capital has to be attributed for taxation purposes only (e.g. based on the equity requirements imposed by the Austrian Banking Act) according to the OECD report on the attribution of profits to permanent establishments dated 17 July 2008

Country					
Belgium	No general thin capitalization rules. A debt-to-equity ratio may apply in the following cases: 7:1 if interest is paid to taxpayers benefiting from a tax regime more advantageous than the Belgian one on the income received and provided certain limits are exceeded 1:1 if interest is paid to a director or a person exercising similar functions and to the extent certain limits are exceeded	No	No	No	N/A
Bulgaria	Yes	Yes	Yes	No	N/A
Cyprus	No	N/A	N/A	No	N/A
Czech Republic	Yes	Yes	No	Yes	The debt-to-equity ratio for banks and insurance companies is 6:1, whereas for other companies the ratio is set at 4:1

Table 5.2 (continued)

Country	1. Do you have thin capitalization rules in your country?	2. Are these thin capitalization rules applicable to related-party interest?	3. Are these thin capitalization rules applicable to third-party interest?	4. Do thin capitalization rules apply to banks?	If your answer to question 4 is yes, please specify, if applicable, the difference between the thin capitalization rules for banks and the thin capitalization rules for companies of other sectors / non-banks
Denmark	Yes	Yes	The calculation of the 4:1 debt-to-equity ratio is made based on all debt in the company. However, only related debt would be subject to limitations	No	N/A
Estonia	No	N/A	N/A	No	N/A
Finland	No	N/A	N/A	No	N/A
France	Yes	Yes	No	No	N/A

Germany	Yes	Yes	Yes	Yes	The German thin capitalization rules are also applicable to banks. However, according to the mechanism of the German interest-capping rules (interest expenses are always tax deductible to the extent they do not exceed interest income earned) banks are typically not burdened by the German thin capitalization rules
Greece	Yes: interest corresponding to loans exceeding the 3:1 debt-to-equity ratio is not tax deductible	Yes	No. However, loans granted by third parties and guaranteed by a related party are taken into account for the calculation of the 3:1 ratio	No	N/A

Table 5.2 (continued)

Country	1. Do you have thin capitalization rules in your country?	2. Are these thin capitalization rules applicable to related-party interest?	3. Are these thin capitalization rules applicable to third-party interest?	4. Do thin capitaliz- ation rules apply to banks?	If your answer to question 4 is yes, please specify, if applicable, the difference between the thin capitalization rules for banks and the thin capitalization rules for companies of other sectors/ non-banks
Hungary	Yes	Yes (except related party in the bank sector)	Yes (except third party in the bank sector)	Yes	For the computation of the debt-to-equity ratio (=3:1), banks do not have to take into consideration their liabilities in connection with their financial services activities, whereas other companies do
Ireland	No (however, certain requalifications may apply when interest payments are made to a 75% non-resident group member)	N/A	N/A	No	N/A

| Italy | No | N/A | N/A | No | Interesting to mention is that interest expenses incurred by banks are deducible at 96%, whereas for companies of other sectors/non-banks, interest expenses are fully deductible provided that they do not exceed specific ratios |

by increased payments by other companies. The transitional problems in moving to a CBIT would be significant, especially when debt is issued in full expectation of deductibility.

5.2.3   An Allowance for Corporate Equity

Countries may also apply positive tax incentive rules to encourage companies to use equity funding. Under an Allowance for Corporate Equity (ACE), companies would retain interest deductibility but also allow a deduction for a notional return on equity. For instance, Brazil has had a CIT with these features for many years. Austria, Croatia and Italy have all had CITs with an element of an ACE. Belgium has recently introduced a notional interest deduction regime, which mainly consists of a tax deduction corresponding to a notional interest cost computed on adjusted equity capital. This regime was introduced with the aim to equilibrate the tax treatment of equity-funded and debt-funded companies. Studies by Staderini (2001), Pricen (2010) and Klemm (2007) review the wider experience with ACE and provide evidence that such schemes have indeed reduced debt financing.[2]

Although the adoption of the ACE would result in revenue loss, the IMF (2010) argues that transitional provisions can limit this. Moreover, the gain would also be less for financial firms than other firms, since they tend to be much more highly geared. The use of an ACE can further be limited by applying the same notional return, which should approximate some risk-free return, to equity, as well as to debt. This would have the further advantage of eliminating any distinction between debt and equity for tax purposes. Table 5.3 gives an overview of ACE around the world.

5.2.4 Other anti-avoidance rules

Not all countries have anti-avoidance rules. It should be noted that in those countries where domestic legislation does set down anti-avoidance rules, they generally apply to all companies, and thus not specifically or solely to banks. In this regard, only the US has reported certain specific anti-avoidance rules applying to the financial sector, and thus to banks, many of which relate to profit offshoring. The case law of the Court of Justice of the European Union has set stringent regulations for the application of these rules.

To summarize, very few countries have enacted specific tax rules to limit interest deductibility by banks. This may be because accepting deposits from customers, and advancing loans, coupled with the payment of interest on those deposits, is the core activity of the retail banking sector. Therefore, there is little tax incentive attached to the deduction of interest payments, as they are more a business characteristic inherent to the retail banking sector; but this does not apply to the wider financial sector.

Table 5.3 Overview of ACE around the world

Country	Period	Name	Base/Rate	Details
Austria	2000–04	Notional interest	Book value of new (post-reform) equity / Average return of government bonds in secondary markets plus 0.8 pp	The notional return is taxed at a reduced rate of 25 per cent instead of 34 per cent
Belgium	Since 2006	Risk capital deduction / notional interest deduction	Book value of equity / Average monthly government bond rate of year preceding fiscal year by two years. Rate capped at 6.5 per cent and cannot change by more than 1 pp from year to year. Special SME rate is 0.5 pp higher	The notional return is deductible

Brazil	Since 1996	Remuneration of equity	Book value of equity / Rate applicable to long-term loans	Up to the level of the notional return, dividends can be paid as 'interest on equity'. This is deductible for all corporate income taxes and subject to the usual withholding tax on interest
Croatia	1994–2000	Protective interest	Book value of equity / 5 per cent plus inflation rate of industrial goods if positive	The notional return is deductible
Italy	1997–2003	Dual income tax	Book value of new (post-reform) equity. From 2000: 120 per cent of new equity. In 2001: 140 per cent of new equity, then again 100 per cent of new equity / 7 per cent 1997–2000, 6 per cent 2001	The notional return is taxed at a reduced rate of 19 per cent. Other profits are taxed at 37 per cent (34 per cent in 2003). Before 2001, the average tax must be at least 27 per cent

Source: This table is adapted from Klemm (2007).

Moreover, the EC (2011) report states that at least one member country felt that banks' funding should be sufficiently regulated using capital and liquidity ratios such that further corrective tax-based measures were unnecessary.

While the application of the above tax proposals to financial institutions might seem tempting, they could create tax arbitraging opportunities. For instance, providing ACE treatment only for banks would require anti-avoidance rules to prevent 'shadow banks' from exploiting the situation. Moreover, changes to personal taxation may also be needed along with these reforms. Nevertheless, although such tax reforms would be difficult to implement, the payoff from reducing the fundamental bias to excess leverage could be substantial.

5.3 Labour taxation

There are generally no differences in the treatment of the personal income of workers employed in the financial sector, except for the introduction of a special bonus tax (EC, 2010), albeit temporary for some EU member states, on financial sector employees. A special enhanced tax on bonuses would lead to higher tax rates than personal income taxation alone. In a limited number of countries, stock options and bonuses benefit from a favourable tax treatment, but this treatment is available across all sectors. In the shadow banking sphere, however, widespread use is made of 'carried interest' taxed at the lower Capital Gain Tax rate.

Using a novel database of executive directors for the period 2002–2007 for both EU and non-EU countries, Egger et al. (2012) show that there is a significant earnings premium in the financial sector, which for the overall sample available (including both EU and non-EU countries) amounts to about 40 per cent after conditioning out observable director-specific and firm-specific characteristics. Nevertheless, considerable heterogeneity of earnings across different types of businesses within the financial sector exists. In fact, one should expect that compensation levels differ sharply between more conservative commercial banks and riskier investment companies. Using the conservative commercial banks as a reference point, they show that individuals in the real estate sector, the insurance sector and a number of other financial businesses earn significantly higher compensation. This finding holds true for the whole sample, as well as for the EU one.

For the US, Philippon and Reshef (2009) use detailed data on wages in the country's financial sector between 1930 and 2006 to identify the existence of economic rents in the sector, which can explain the wage differential of 30 to 50 per cent. They provide evidence that these wages reached excessively high levels, especially around 1930 and between 1995 and 2006. On the one hand, their results suggest that complex corporate activities such as Initial Public Offerings or credit risk have a positive effect on the demand for skilled workers, whereas on the other hand, stricter regulation has a negative effect on the demand for skilled workers.

Notes

1. The IMF (2010) notes that there are possibilities beyond those listed here, such as movement to 'cash flow' forms of CIT.
2. An overview of the design issues of ACE can be found in OECD (2007) and IMF (2009).

6. Taxation of financial instruments

The IMF (2010) argues that there may be reasons to consider additional, more permanent tax measures beyond a special bank levy. This is because the large fiscal, economic and social costs of financial crises, and implicit insurance by taxpayers, may require a contribution from the financial sector to general revenues beyond covering the fiscal costs of direct support. Moreover, taxes might have a role in correcting adverse externalities arising from the financial sector, such as the creation of systemic risks and excessive risk taking.

Specifically, proposals include taxes on: short-term and/or foreign exchange borrowing; on high rates of return to offset any tendency for decision takers to attach too little weight to downside risks; and corrective taxes related to systemic risks and interconnectedness. The prevailing view is that receipts from these taxes would contribute to general revenue and that they need not equal the damage that they seek to limit or avert.[1]

Explicitly corrective taxes, on systemic risk for instance, would need to be considered in close coordination with regulatory charges to assure capital and liquidity adequacy. The remainder of this chapter focuses on two possible instruments directed largely to revenue generation,[2] although in each case their behavioural, and hence potentially corrective or distortionary, impact cannot be ignored.

6.1 Financial Transactions Tax

From the beginning of the financial crisis, the design and implementation of an FTT have received much support from various circles of society, including the 'occupy' protesters, policy makers and academics. According to the EC (2010) report, the financial sector might be too large and take excessive risks because of actual or expected state support. As a result of this moral hazard problem, the financial market is very volatile and this creates negative external effects for the rest of the economy. The EC argues that an FTT might be used as a corrective tool for this moral hazard, thereby enhancing the potential efficiency and stability of financial markets.

The IMF (2010) argues that various proposals for some form of FTT differ, including its goals and degrees of detail. For instance, one particular form is a 'Tobin tax' (Tobin, 1978) on foreign exchange transactions. This would be an internationally uniform tax on all spot conversions of one currency into another, proportional to the size of the transaction. The underlying presumption is that the tax would deter short-term financial 'round trip' currency conversions, or wasteful 'over-trading'. Tobin (1978) proposes that each government would administrate the tax over its own jurisdiction and the tax revenues could be paid to the IMF or World Bank. Although he recognizes that 'ingenious patterns of evasion' would occur in response to the tax, he argues that the benefit would outweigh the costs. He postulates that the disadvantages are small compared with the inefficiency and wastefulness of the current system.

Tobin's proposal on exchange rates remains very informative for today's debate on a general FTT, and indeed Tobin (1984) extended the argument for applying an FTT to the trading of financial instruments, and not just currencies. As the IMF (2010) states, the common feature focused on here is the applicability of the tax to a very wide range of potentially wasteful transactions. More specifically, an FTT would be applied to all financial transactions and particularly to those carried out in organized markets (Schamp, 2011). The EC (2010) states that it would be levied each time the underlying asset is traded at a relatively low statutory rate; minimizing distortions while generating potentially considerable revenue. Advocates of an FTT argue that its implementation would raise substantial revenue: it has been estimated that a tax of one

basis point would raise over $200 billion annu-
ally if levied globally on stocks, bonds and
derivative transactions; and a 0.5 basis point
Tobin tax on spot and derivative transactions in
the four major trading currencies would raise
$20–40 billion (IMF, 2010). Moreover, Schul-
meister et al. (2008) estimate that the revenue of
a global FTT would amount to 1.52 per cent of
world GDP at a tax rate of 0.1 per cent. In the
EU, it is estimated that tax revenues would be 2.1
per cent of GDP if a similar tax were imposed.[3]

Furthermore, an FTT cannot be dismissed on
the grounds of administrative impracticability. In
fact, as the IMF (2010) notes, most G20 countries,
including the UK, already tax some financial
transactions. For instance, Argentina, which has
the broadest coverage, taxes payments into and
from current accounts, and in Turkey all the
receipts of banks and insurance companies are
taxed. Other countries charge particular financial
transactions, such as the 0.5 per cent stamp duty
on locally registered share purchases in the
United Kingdom, and there is also a stamp duty
charge on house purchases. As experience with
UK stamp duty on share purchases shows, col-
lecting taxes on a wide range of exchange-traded
securities, and possibly also financial derivatives,
could be straightforward and cheap if levied
through central clearing mechanisms.

Nevertheless, some important practical issues
have not yet been fully resolved. For instance, it
might be expected that an FTT might drive

transactions into less secure channels; but there is a post-crisis countervailing regulatory requirement to require more financial instrument transactions to be undertaken through exchanges with central counterparties and clearing. However, implementation difficulties are not unique to the FTT, and a sufficient basis exists for practical implementation of at least some form of the tax to focus on the central question of whether there would be any substantial costs from implementing an FTT.

France and Italy introduced an FTT on 1 August 2012 and 1 March 2013, respectively. The FTT in France is a tax on equity transactions, high-frequency trading in equities and 'naked' exposure in credit default swap (CDS)[4] in EU sovereign debt. In Italy, it is broader in scope and taxes equities, equity-like financial instruments and derivatives, and high-frequency trading. The FTT in France is quite similar to UK stamp duty, apart from: the higher rate of 0.2 per cent, although it had been 0.1 per cent before February 2013; the exclusion of companies with a market capitalization of less than €1 billion; and the fact that it is applied to the broker, dealer or custodian at the time of settlement, as opposed to the buyer in the case of UK stamp duty. Furthermore, the French FTT also taxes high-frequency trading in equities and 'naked' CDS exposures in EU sovereign debt.

Initial evidence[5] shows that the FTT in France and Italy has reduced volume and liquidity in the market. The French FTT has also failed to raise the expected revenue due to reduction in the volume of over-the-counter (OTC) transactions. In the available academic literature, there is consensus that the French STT (Securities Transaction Tax) has reduced traded values and turnover (Capelle-Blancard and Havrylchyk, 2013; Colliard and Hoffmann, 2013; Meyer et al., 2013; Parwada et al., 2013); however, the evidence on liquidity and volatility is mixed. Parwada et al. (2013) and Haferkorn and Zimmermann (2013) give empirical evidence of reduction in liquidity while Capelle-Blancard and Havrylchyk (2013) and Meyer et al. (2013) find no evidence of reduction in liquidity with the introduction of the French STT. The impact of the STT is statistically insignificant in the studies by Capelle-Blancard and Havrylchyk (2013), Colliard and Hoffmann (2013) and Haferkorn and Zimmermann (2013) while Becchetti et al. (2013) give evidence of negative effect of the STT on volatility (see Capelle-Blancard, 2014 for detail).

The originally proposed EU FTT is broader than UK, French and Italian stamp duty, in the sense that it taxes cash and derivatives across all asset classes, with the exception of spot foreign exchange. The EU FTT proposal was to levy 0.1 per cent on stock and bond trades and 0.01 per cent on derivatives. It was to be applicable on any transaction involving one financial institution with its headquarters in the tax area, or trading on behalf of a client based in the tax area. However, to date (22 October 2014) the participating member states are struggling to make much progress, despite the expression of their desire to see real progress with the proposed EU FTT earlier in 2014. The arguments surround the scope and the revenue allocation. For the scope, it is not clear whether it will have a narrow scope similar to existing French and Italian FTTs or a broad scope as advocated by the German Government. Next, whether the residence or issuance principle should prevail as far as the implementation scope of the tax is concerned. Under the residence principle, the FTT will be applicable to transactions entered into by a financial institution resident in the FTT area, even if the subject assets are not from the FTT area, while the issuance principle is much like UK stamp duty or the French and Italian FTTs, where the FTT will be applicable to transactions on assets issued by a financial institution in the FTT area. Regarding the revenue allocation, no agreement has been reached on alternative allocation models and potential sharing of models.

Critics were of the view that such a generally applied FTT would damage the repo market, which is important for interbank financing and as a conduit for central bank monetary policy implementation, because it taxes on both buy and sell legs of repo, and reverse repo, trades. Repo trades also play an important role in clearing of activities, collateralization of payments between banks, and provision of market liquidity for smaller currency areas.

6.1.1   *Some advantages and disadvantages of implementing FTT*[6]

Proponents of an FTT argue that its implementation has significant revenue potential. However, the actual amount raised greatly depends on the design of the tax. For instance, the level of collection has a major influence on revenue raised (Schamp, 2011). Therefore, tax collection at the level of the trading markets would target only a small proportion of financial transactions, given the fragmentation of the trading landscape and the growing importance of OTC derivatives (UN, 2010), although this has been reversed by legislation in the US and the EU requiring exchange trading of most derivatives. In addition, tax revenue depends on the base and rate of the FTT. Nevertheless, the United Nations' high-level Advisory Group on Climate Change Financing calculated that the amount of revenue would be significant, even with a very low tax rate.

Moreover, an FTT is an innovative source of financing (EC, 2010). This means that no money is extracted from other budgets. Therefore, the considerable revenues collected could be used for the achievement of policy goals on a supranational level. For instance, global public goods, such as development aid or climate control, could be financed (Schamp, 2011). Alternatively, the revenue raised could be hypothecated to fund bank resolution regimes and regulation and supervision.

The implementation of an FTT would be accompanied by administrative, monitoring and collection costs. However, as discussed previously with regard to the experience in the United Kingdom, if the tax is properly designed, then the administrative costs can be negligible. For instance, in the UK a tax is levied on electronic paperless share transactions purchases, called the Stamp Duty Reserve Tax. In this case, collection is made through the electronic transaction system of the London Stock Exchange and the cost is remarkably low, that is, 0.2 pence per pound sterling of revenue collected (Schamp, 2011).

In fact, Schamp (2011) argues that the implementation of the FTT is rather simple and that it could be operational quickly. Moreover, the proposed FTT can build on past experiences of transaction taxes and financial infrastructures, which can operate as central points. To conclude, as the UN states, in this respect 'the implementation of an FTT is not a question of feasibility, although strong will is necessary to oppose traditional objections' (UN, 2010, p. 6). However, during the G20 summit in Toronto (June 2010), the finance ministers decided that a global FTT was no longer feasible.

Turning to the potential disadvantages, the IMF (2010) argues that an FTT is 'not the best way to finance a resolution mechanism', as the volume of transactions is not a good proxy for either the benefits it conveys to particular institutions or the costs they are likely to impose on it. Moreover, it is not focused on the core sources of financial instability, as it would not target any of the key attributes that give rise to systemic risk: institution size, interconnectedness and substitutability. Adjusting the tax rate to reflect such considerations would be possible in principle, but highly complex in practice. The IMF (2010) states that if the aim is to discourage particular types of transactions, taxing or regulating them directly could do this more effectively.

Moreover, Schamp (2011) notes that if the implementation of the FTT were limited to a few jurisdictions, it would be unlikely to raise the revenue sought, because avoidance of the trading market subject to the transaction tax would result in a substantial decrease in the tax base. Nevertheless, the UN (2010) and Cortez and Vogel (2011) argue that the implementation of an FTT in all major financial centres would be sufficient to prevent avoidance, as liquidity and legal requirements are still decisive factors and in many tax havens transaction costs are much higher compared with industrialized countries. In contrast, a global application is needed to ensure a worldwide playing field for global financial players.

Even if an FTT were implemented, Schamp (2011) argues that it is likely that investors would demand a higher minimum rate of return on their investment, given the rise in transaction costs and hence the expectation of a decrease in future profits. Since the cost of capital for a company is influenced by the minimum rate of return demanded by investors, the introduction of an FTT might increase the cost of capital for companies. Therefore, the impact of the FTT on a company's cost of capital will depend on the frequency with which its equity securities are traded. For this scenario, Bond et al. (2004) find that after stamp duty in the UK was halved in 1986, share price increases depended on market turnover. As a consequence of the increased cost of capital, fewer investment projects will be profitable, and hence investment and economic growth in the economy will be hampered (Schamp, 2011). However, Cortez and Vogel (2011) argue that the increase in the cost of capital could be ameliorated if the government issued fewer bonds as a result of the additional revenue raised by the FTT. This in turn would increase the demand for non-government securities.

Most importantly, the real burden of the FTT may fall largely on final consumers, rather than, as often seems to be supposed, earnings in the financial sector. Although, undoubtedly, some of the tax would be borne by the owners and managers of financial institutions, a large part of this burden may well be passed on to the users of financial services (both businesses and individuals) in the form of reduced returns on savings or higher costs of borrowing.[7] According to the IMF (2010), this is because an FTT is levied on every transaction, so the cumulative, 'cascading' effects of the tax, charged on values that reflect the payment of tax at earlier stages, can be significant and non-transparent. Moreover, it is not obvious that the incidence would fall mainly on either the better off or financial sector *rentiers*.[8] In sum, since the incidence of an FTT remains unclear, it should not be thought of as a well-targeted way of taxing any rents earned in the financial sector.

Further, the IMF (2010) argues that care should be taken in assessing the potential efficiency of an FTT in raising revenue, because[9] FTT taxes transactions between businesses; including indirectly through the impact on the prices of non-financial products. The argument that an FTT would cause little distortion because it would be levied at a very low rate on a very broad base is not very persuasive. In fact, a central principle of public finance is that if the sole policy objective is to raise revenue, then taxing transactions between businesses, which many financial transactions do, is unwise because distorting business decisions reduces total output; while taxing that output directly can raise more taxes. Technically, a tax levied on transactions at one stage 'cascades' into prices at all further stages of production. Hence, for instance, most countries have

found that VAT, which effectively excludes transactions between businesses, is a more efficient
revenue raiser than turnover or transactions
taxes.[10] For revenue raising, there are more efficient instruments than an FTT.

Further, experience shows that financial transactions seem to be particularly vulnerable to
avoidance or evasion. For instance, in the United
Kingdom 'contracts for differences' are used to
avoid the tax. A 'contract for difference' is a
financial product which reallocates the income
associated with share of ownership, without
changing the ownership itself. However, to mitigate the incentive for such engineering, the tax
rate could be set lower than the avoidance costs
and tax authorities could react by incorporating
new financial instruments in the tax base
(Schamp, 2011).

Finally, Schamp (2011) notes that national and
international legal constraints should be considered. The underlying belief is that the host country of the financial infrastructure should collect
the proposed FTT on behalf of the international
community. Therefore, at the national level, parliamentary authorization to collect the tax is
necessary and a legal scheme should be designed
for collection. Additionally, the compatibility of
the FTT with the EU free movement of capital
directive should be assessed.

There is general consensus in the empirical
literature that an FTT reduces market volume
and liquidity and increases market volatility and

the cost of capital (Amihud and Mendelson, 1992; Umlauf, 1993; Jones and Seguin, 1997; Baltagi et al., 2006; Bloomfield et al., 2009; Pomeranets and Weaver, 2011). The study by Pomeranets and Weaver (2011) examines changes in market quality associated with nine modifications to the New York State STT between 1932 and 1981. They find that the New York STT increased individual stock volatility, widened bid–ask spreads, increased price impact and decreased volume on the New York Stock Exchange.

There is also the notorious example of an FTT in Sweden in 1984, which introduced a 1 per cent tax on equity transactions, which it increased to 2 per cent in 1986. The purpose of the tax was the same as that of the EU FTT: to raise revenue and to improve the efficiency of the market by reducing speculative transactions. Umlauf (1993) studied the impact of these changes on the Swedish market and found that stock prices and turnover declined after an increase in the rate of FTT to 2 per cent in 1986. Trading volume fell by 30 per cent, and 60 per cent of the 11 most traded shares migrated to London to avoid the tax. In 1989, the scope of the tax was broadened to include bonds, which led to 85 per cent and 98 per cent reductions in bond trading volume and bond derivatives trading volume, respectively. The tax reduced the liquidity of the markets but did not reduce their volatility. Table 6.1 gives an overview of STT around the world.

Table 6.1 Overview of STT around the world

Country	Securities Transaction Taxes Applicable in Principle	On Regulated Markets	Type of Securities in Scope	Rate	Revenue	Remarks
Belgium	Tax on stock exchange transactions	Yes	All securities	0.17% (or 0.5% or 0.07% depending on the type of security)	EUR 134 million	There is an exemption for non-residents and the financial sector acting for its own account

Table 6.1 (continued)

Country	Securities Transaction Taxes Applicable in Principle	On Regulated Markets	Type of Securities in Scope	Rate	Revenue	Remarks
Cyprus	Levy on transactions effected in respect of securities listed at the Cypriot Stock Exchange	Yes	'Titles', meaning shares, stocks, debentures, founding and other titles of companies that are listed at the Stock Exchange	0.15%	EUR 1.4 million	This legislation ceases to be of effect from 31 December 2011
	Stamp duty	No, exempt if listed at Stock Exchange	Securities issued by Cypriot-resident companies	0.15% (on the first EUR 170,860) plus 0.2% (on amounts over 170,860)	N/A	Stamp duty is applicable to the agreement and not to the transaction
Finland	Transfer tax	No, exempt if traded on a qualifying market	Finnish securities, e.g. equities, PPL (Paper Products Ltd) stock options, but not debt securities or derivatives	1.60%	N/A	

| France | STT | Yes | Transactions on shares of publicly traded companies established in France, whose capital is over EUR 1 billion. High-frequency and automated trading operations, taxable at a rate of 0.01% on the amount of cancelled or modified orders above a ceiling, which will be defined by a Ministerial Decree; and Purchase of a Credit Default Swap (CDS) by a French company, taxable at a rate of 0.01% on the amount | 0.1% for shares, 0.01% for High-Frequency Trading (HFT) and CDS | N/A | The French Securities Transaction Tax is in effect from 1 August 2012 |

Table 6.1 (continued)

Country	Securities Transaction Taxes Applicable in Principle	On Regulated Markets	Type of Securities in Scope	Rate	Revenue	Remarks
Greece	Transaction duty	Yes, OTC transfers of Greek-listed shares are subject to the duty	Greek- or foreign-listed shares and compound products such as equity swaps, call options, futures	0.15%	EUR 54 million in 2010	Draft bill in which amendments are proposed, e.g. abolition of transaction duty for the sale of listed shares initially acquired after 1 January 2012
Ireland	Stamp duty		Stocks or marketable securities (including derivatives) of an Irish company or Irish immovable property	1% but possibly up to 6%	N/A	

Italy	FTT	Yes	Shares, equity-like financial instruments and derivatives, as well as high-frequency trading	0.10% per exchange transaction and 0.20% on over-the-counter trades	N/A	The Italian Securities Transaction Tax is in effect from 1 March 2013
Poland	Taxation of sale or exchange of property rights	No, exemption for transactions within an organized market	Securities and derivatives, except Polish treasury bonds, etc.	1.00%	N/A	
Romania	Securities transaction taxes	Yes, whether on the regulated market or not	All types of securities	A commission of an EUR maximum of 0.08% or a monitoring fee of 0.15%; a commision of 0.10 RON when derivatives are involved	EUR 4,022 million in 2009	

Table 6.1 (continued)

Country	Securities Transaction Taxes Applicable in Principle	On Regulated Markets	Type of Securities in Scope	Rate	Revenue	Remarks
UK	Stamp duty and Stamp Duty Reserve Tax		Equities, certain equity derivatives (cash-settled derivatives excluded) and some loans having equity-like features	0.5% (or 1.5%)	N/A	Certain recognized intermediaries (financial sector traders) are given an exemption
Singapore	Stamp duty	No, not applicable to transactions on the Singapore Exchange via the scripless settlement system	Stocks and shares, including debt with certain features	0.20%	EUR 1,157 million in 2007	

| Switzerland | Transfer stamp tax | Yes | Bonds, shares (including shares in investment funds) | 0.15% for domestic securities and 0.3% for foreign securities | Foreign banks and securities dealers are exempt parties, among others |

Source: Part of this table is adapted from EC (2011).

6.2 Financial Activities Tax

As an alternative to an FTT, the IMF (2010) proposes the implementation of an FAT levied on the sum of profits and remuneration of financial institutions, although the two taxes are not mutually exclusive. Since aggregate value added is the sum of profits and remuneration, an FAT in effect taxes the net transactions of financial institutions, whereas an FTT taxes gross transactions. However, like an FTT, an FAT would, in the absence of special arrangements, tax business transactions because no credit would be given to their customers for an FAT paid by financial institutions. Alternative definitions of profits and remuneration for inclusion in the base of an FAT would enable it to be used in pursuit of a range of objectives.[11] For instance, with the inclusion of all remuneration, the IMF (2010) argues that an FAT would effectively be a tax on value added, and so would partially offset the risk of the financial sector becoming unduly large as a result of its treatment under existing VAT arrangements, where financial services are exempt. Moreover, to avoid aggravating distortions, the tax rate would need to be below current standard VAT rates. Because financial services are commonly VAT exempt, the financial sector may be under-taxed and hence perhaps 'too big', relative to other sectors. In fact, the size of the gross financial sector value added in many countries suggests that even a relatively low-rate

FAT could raise significant revenue in a fair and reasonably efficient way. For instance, the IMF (2010) report shows that, in the UK, a 5 per cent FAT, with all salaries and bonuses included in the base, might raise about 0.3 per cent of GDP. Moreover, the IMF (2010) argues that with the inclusion only of profits above some acceptable threshold rate of return, an FAT would become a tax on 'excessive' returns, or rents, in the financial sector. The underlying belief is that it would mitigate the excessive risk taking that can arise from the undervaluation by private sector decision makers of losses in bad times, because they are expected to be borne by others, or 'socialized', since it would reduce the after-tax return in good times.[12] It should be noted that there might be more effective tax and/or regulatory ways to do this.

The IMF (2010) also states that the implementation of an FAT should be relatively straightforward, as it would draw on the practices of established taxes. Naturally, there would be technical issues to resolve, but the IMF argues that most are of a kind with which tax administrations are used to dealing. Even though there would be difficulties in the potential shifting of profits and remuneration to low-tax jurisdictions, a low-rate FAT might not add greatly to current incentives for tax avoidance, and might not greatly change them if adopted at broadly similar rates in a range of countries.

An FAT would tend to reduce the size of the financial sector and will fall on intermediate transactions. Hence its implementation does not directly distort the activities of the financial institutions and because an FAT is essentially a levy on economic rents, it would tend to reduce the size of the sector without changing its activities. The IMF (2010) argues that in many respects an FAT has the nature of VAT in the sense that there would be no direct impact on the structure of the activities undertaken by financial institutions themselves, as liability depends on profit, not on how it is earned or on the volume of turnover. Of course, there would be a major difference from VAT, in that the tax would fall on businesses rather than directly on final consumers.

Shaviro (2012) also favours an FAT over an FTT because of the broad 'net' measure of FAT compared with a narrow 'gross' measure of financial sector activity. The Parliamentary Commission on Banking Standards (PCBS, 2013b) report also quotes different parties who prefer an FAT over an FTT for three reasons: it is less easily avoidable through relocations; incidence is more certain; and it would generate the same amount of revenue with fewer distortions.

6.3 VAT on financial services

A VAT (or Government Sales Tax, GST) is a consumption tax that is collected on the value added at each stage of production. This is different from a Retail Sales Tax, which is charged on sales to final consumers. In order to understand a VAT on financial services, it is important to distinguish between the purchase of financial services by businesses and consumers. The literature concludes (Firth and McKenzie, 2012) that purchases of financial services by businesses should not be subject to VAT, whereas for purchases by consumers the answer is not so clear. Firth and McKenzie (2012) observe that the non-taxation of intermediate financial transactions with businesses can be achieved in two fundamental ways. If VAT is levied on the purchase of a financial service, regardless of whether or not the underlying price is explicit or implicit by way of the margin (and ignoring measurement issues with regard to the latter for now; this issue will be discussed below), the business should obtain a full input credit for the VAT paid on the service, and the financial institution providing the service should obtain full credit for the VAT paid on the inputs purchased to produce the service. If no VAT is levied on the transaction, then the VAT levied on the inputs used by the financial intermediary to provide the service to businesses should still be fully credited on the part of the financial intermediary, achieving 'zero rating'.

It is important to note that it is a very common practice to exempt financial products and services from VAT, meaning that the tax is not charged to the consumer but tax paid on related inputs is not recovered. Therefore financial services are effectively 'input taxed'. On one hand, the reason behind the implementation of VAT exemption on financial services lies in the conceptual difficulty that arises when payment for service is implicit in an interest rate spread, between borrowing and lending rates, for instance. Taxing the overall spread may be easy, but proper operation of the VAT requires some way of allocating that tax between the two sides of the transaction so as to ensure that registered businesses receive a credit, but final consumers do not.

On the other hand, exemption means that business use of financial services tends to be over-taxed, but use by final consumers is under-taxed. Hence prices charged by the financial institutions are likely to reflect the unrecovered VAT charged on their inputs, so that business users will pay more than they would have in the absence of the VAT. Generally, the credit mechanism of the VAT ensures that it does not affect prices paid by registered users on their purchase. But exemption means that this is not so, either for financial institutions themselves, or their customers, or, through further cascading, the customers of their customers. Of course, this runs counter to the principle underlying the VAT, that transactions between businesses should not be taxed unless doing so addresses some clear market failure. Moreover, exemption for final consumers is likely to mean under-taxation, since the price they pay does not reflect the full value added by financial service providers, but only their use of taxable inputs. Further, cheaper financial services may encourage over-consumption of them. Why should there be a low rate of VAT on the use of financial services? Atkinson and Stiglitz (1976) and Mirrlees et al. (2011, Chapter 6) argue for taxation of financial services at a relatively low rate so that favourable treatment helps counteract the general tendency of taxation to discourage work effort. Since the adoption of the Sixth EC VAT Directive in 1977 (Article 135 (1) of the VAT Directive), the EU's common value-added tax system has generally exempted mainstream financial services, including insurance and investment funds.

The Directive reflects an uncertain approach, in that it allows EU member states the option of taxing financial services. However, the difficulty arises of technically defining the price for specific financial operations. Studies such as those by Kerrigan (2010) and Mirrlees et al. (2011, Chapter 8), provide a detailed discussion of the problem of VAT on financial services, arguing that around two-thirds of all financial services are margin based; which complicates the implementation of the invoice-credit VAT system. Nevertheless, this difficulty seems to be surmountable. For instance, in Germany, where the granting of loans is subject to VAT under the Directive's option to tax, an acceptable methodology seems to have been found to tax these margin-based operations.[13] Yet, the extent to which applying VAT to the financial sector (and its clients) would raise additional tax revenues and, consequently, the extent to which the exemption constitutes a tax advantage for the financial sector, remains an unsettled empirical question. Known as the 'irrecoverable VAT problem', the exemption means that the financial sector does not charge VAT on most of its output, so it cannot deduct the VAT charged on its input. Estimates by Genser and Winker (1997) for Germany (7 billion DM for 1994), Huizinga (2002) for the EU15 (12 billion EUR for 1998 or 0.15 per cent of GDP) and the UK Treasury[14] for the UK (£9.05 billion or about 0.6 per cent of GDP) indicate that there might be a sizeable tax advantage (measured as VAT not collected). Arguments are also put forth that claim that irrecoverable VAT is the largest tax burden for the sector.

The EC (2011) report presents a new estimate of the magnitude of the problem. The calculations are based on European Sector Accounts on the consumption of financial services by sectors, in which data restricted to financial intermediation and other tax-exempt financial services are not covered. By applying methodologies proposed by Huizinga (2002) and Lockwood (2010), the data are used to estimate the potential advantage for the financial sector from VAT exemption.

Table 6.2 presents three estimations where the difference between them is the data basis for the calculation of the irrecoverable VAT, which in the case of a VAT application would be fully deductible. The most reliable estimates are from estimation (1), where the intermediate consumption of the financial intermediation can be directly measured using an input-output table. Although the data are very rough approximations and should be interpreted with caution, the estimates suggest that VAT exemption leads to an advantage for the financial sector in the range of 0.11 per cent to 0.17 per cent of GDP (the results are in line with the results of Huizinga (2002) of around 0.15 per cent of GDP). Overall, the results indicate that the VAT exemption of financial services might be an advantage for the financial sector. The EC (2011) report notes that the results do not change significantly when other estimates for the irrecoverable VAT based on sector account data are used.

It should further be noted that all three estimates do not take into account the behavioural response due to price changes when applying VAT to financial services. Although the inclusion of the financial sector in VAT would indeed lead to price changes, such changes should be seen as the correction to an existing distortion, rather than a new distortion. The reason is that alongside the question of whether VAT on financial services would raise revenues, there is an economic distortion arising from the current VAT exemption. While services provided to households are too cheap, services to businesses are more expensive, leading to a misallocation of the consumption of financial services.

Moreover, it can be deduced (following IMF, 2010) that the net impact of exemption is likely to be less tax revenue and a larger financial sector. Evidence suggests that revenue would be increased by taxing the final use of financial services at the standard VAT rate (Genser and Winkler, 1997; Huizinga, 2002). At the same time, the effect on the size of the sector depends on the relative price sensitivities of business and final use, even though the same evidence creates some presumption that the exemption of many financial services under current VAT results in the financial sector being larger, with more household consumption of financial services, than it would be under a single rate VAT.

However, Grubert and Mackie (2000) argue that financial services are not purchased for their consumption value but rather to facilitate final consumption and should not be taxed. Boadway and Keen (2003) argue that there are many goods and services that one would question should be taxed using a VAT. They all have a similar characteristic because they are a means to an end rather than ends in themselves, and are therefore intermediate transactions. Indeed, virtually every good may be thought of in those terms, in the sense that they are inputs into some notion of well being or production process, but the idea of VAT is to concentrate on the value added. As per the Corlett-Hague (1953) rule, to minimize the costs of distortions caused by the tax system, goods that are more complementary with the consumption of leisure, which is generally viewed as being non-taxable, should be taxed at higher rates. Since financial services are exempt from VAT, they are implicitly considered equivalent to a necessity, with a view not to pass on the tax burden to the final consumer. In sum, VAT exemption results in the preferential treatment of the financial sector compared with other sectors of the economy, as well as in distortions of prices.

New Zealand and Australia have been put forward as having a more efficient and a fair model that seems to avoid some of the potential distortive impacts of the implementation of VAT. New Zealand introduced a uniform GST in 1986 and considered it efficient because of relatively fewer exemptions than in the UK and the EU. Dickson and White (2012) describe the compliance and administrative costs of GST as regressive; however, relief to the poor strata of society is provided via the income tax and social welfare systems. As reported by PWC (2006), in New Zealand, although exemption is afforded to many supplies of financial services, these supplies can be zero rated (at the option of the supplier) when made to principally taxable persons.[15] This guarantees that financial service providers can recover a substantial or significant GST incurred on inputs purchased from third-party suppliers.

In addition, in New Zealand GST exemption does not include non-life insurance, provision of advisory services, equipment leasing, creditor protection policies and some other financial intermediation services. However, transactions dealing with money, issuance of securities, provision of credit and loans, and provision of life insurance remain exempted (Poddar and Kalita, 2010). The New Zealand system of taxation of non-life insurance would seem to have been followed in a number of other countries, including South Africa and Australia.[16] It taxes gross premiums, but gives insurers the ability to reclaim deemed input tax on indemnification of payments, whether or not made to GST-registered insured parties. In this case, the model uses taxes on insurers' cash flows as a surrogate for value added.

The narrow definition of financial services, in the form of Business-to-Business or Business-to-Consumer transactions, has made many which otherwise would have been exempt, taxable. The exemption does not apply to brokering and facilitating services; it includes only borrowing and lending. With respect to Australia, the exemption approach to financial services applies in principle so that a denial of input credit entitlement arises for GST incurred on related costs. In spite of this, the distortive impact of the input credit provision is mitigated by what is termed the Reduced Input Tax Credit (RITC) scheme. This scheme, a unique feature of the

Australian GST code, allows suppliers of financial services to recover 75 per cent of tax paid on
specified inputs. RITC was chosen because of the
significant proportion of labour costs typically
incurred in providing the RITC services. The
main objective of the RITC scheme is to eliminate
the bias to vertical integration, or the self-
supplying of inputs to avoid paying GST to
suppliers, and to facilitate outsourcing, from a
cost efficiency perspective. The inputs that give
rise to a RITC are itemized in regulations, but
broadly include the following: transaction banking and cash management services; payment and
fund transfer services; securities transaction services; loan services; debt collection services;
funds management services; insurance brokerage
and claims-handling services; trustee and custo-
dial services; and supplies for which financial
supply facilitators are paid a commission.

A PWC (2006) report identifies advantages and
disadvantages associated with the implementation of the RITC mechanisms.

Advantages of the Australian RITC scheme
are: that it removes the necessity to make supplies to financial institutions VAT exempt and
hence tax compliance is easier for suppliers to
financial institutions, which remain fully taxable;
it is the recipients' responsibility to determine
the RITC rather than placing the burden on the
suppliers; and the RITC scheme is compatible
with the existing VAT framework (i.e. direct attri-
bution and allocation). For instance, the RITC

can apply to supplies used for taxable and exempt purposes. The recipient then works out the extent of taxable use (an apportionment is made) and then applies the reduced input tax credit to the extent of exempt use. To put this in figures, if an entity makes 50 per cent taxable and 50 per cent exempt supplies, then it can claim back 87.5 per cent of the GST incurred by applying RITC (say 75 per cent) to the remaining 50 per cent exempt use (PWC, 2006).

Disadvantages of the Australian RITC regime are: clear definitions and guidance are needed to identify when the RITC will apply and to what kinds of goods/services; the mechanism requires unanimous support from all States and Territories before the law can be amended – a similar principle applies in the EU; before a RITC can be applied, an apportionment is required to overhead expenditure; it is the recipient that makes an apportionment between taxable and exempt use and then applies the RITC, thereby allowing a RITC to manipulate the apportionment in favour of taxable use to maximize input VAT recovery; it does not apply to all services that may lead to irrecoverable input VAT, for instance it may not apply to the recharge of shared service centre costs from a group company (but outside the GST group); and there is no scientific way of determining RITC as the credit of 75 per cent was chosen after consultation with the industry. Hence, it is difficult to know what the correct RITC should be. In any case, it was agreed that if the service was provided in-house, there should be a GST cost on overheads and some directly attributable costs, and therefore a 100 per cent credit would be inappropriate.

Although some of these services may qualify for exemption in their own right under the Sixth EU VAT Directive, the RITC scheme is an interesting concept and may contribute to the elimination of the bias against outsourcing inherent in other systems.

Financial services are exempt from VAT in the EU and banks do not charge any VAT on their financial services, nor do they recover VAT paid on their business inputs. However, there are some exceptions of specified fee-based services, such as safety deposit box fees, financial advisory services and the zero rating of exported financial services. The Canadian GST is generally similar to the European one with regard to exemption of financial services. However, there is a list of fee-based services that is taxed.[17] The Canadian GST is a credit-invoice tax rather than a subtraction method tax, which was once proposed in Canada (Schenk, 2010).

The cases of Israel and Argentina are severe, in the sense that they arguably over-tax many financial services. First, financial services are exempt from VAT, meaning that financial institutions cannot recover the VAT paid on their purchases, and, secondly, banks are required to pay tax on the aggregate of their wages and profits (Schenk and Oldman, 2007). In order to

Table 6.2   VAT option to tax, payroll taxes and insurance premium tax

Country (April 2011)	Option to Tax	Payroll Tax (Similar to Payroll Tax Base of FAT)	Others
Austria	Option to tax adopted to a very limited extent, i.e. for certain very specific financial services mentioned in article 135 (1) (b) and (c) of Directive 2006/112/EC		
Belgium	Option for taxation adopted to a very limited extent, i.e. for certain very specified financial services mentioned in article 135 (1) (d) of Directive 2006/112/EC		
Bulgaria	Option for taxation adopted to a very limited extent, i.e. for certain very specific financial services mentioned in article 135 (1) (b) of Directive 2006/112/EC		

| Denmark | N/A | Most VAT-exempt activities, including VAT-exempt financial activities, are liable to a Special Payroll Tax.

Also branches and representative offices are liable if they have employees in Denmark.

Financial service companies (or companies whose main activity is financial services) must pay the highest tax rate, namely 10.5% of the payroll related to VAT-exempt activities. The taxable base will as a main rule include all payroll and all taxable benefits |
|---|---|---|
| Estonia | Option for taxation adopted for financial services mentioned in article 135 (1) (b) to (g) of Directive 2006/112/EC | |

Table 6.2 (continued)

Country (April 2011)	Option to Tax	Payroll Tax (Similar to Payroll Tax Base of FAT)	Others
France	The scope of the option is widely defined by a legal provision. However, another provision explicitly excludes from that scope a series of transactions or of kinds of transactions	Not applicable to transactions but paid by a French-established employer on the salaries (progressive in accordance of salary threshold) to the extent that its turnover is either VAT exempt (without credit) or outside the scope of VAT. In this respect, the Payroll Tax is apportioned on the basis of the following ratio: Numerator: the VAT exempt and the outside scope of VAT revenue, and Denominator: the total revenue (taxable, VAT exempt and outside scope of VAT)	Turnover tax: A 'value-added contribution' is assessed on the added value of French companies. This applies to banks and other companies where turnover exceeds EUR 152,500. The tax is computed by applying a progressive rate ranging between 0% and 1.5% on the added value of the company. Both turnover and the added value are calculated according to special provisions for banks (e.g. 95% of dividends deriving from long-term investments are not taken into account instead of a complete exemption)

Germany	Option for taxation adopted for financial services mentioned in article 135 (1) (b) to (f) of Directive 2006/112/EC
	Not applicable for insurance transactions according to article 135 (1) (a) of Directive 2006/112/EC and management of special investment funds according to article 135 (1) (g) of Directive 2006/112/EC
Lithuania	Option for taxation adopted to a limited extent, i.e. for certain very specified financial services mentioned in article 135 (1) (b) to (e) of Directive 2006/112/EC

Source: This table is adapted from EC (2011).

contain inflationary pressures, or for that matter to reduce the wasteful use of financial services, Argentina taxes gross interest on loans under a VAT at different rates. The VAT on these loans to registered businesses is creditable (Schenk and Oldman, 2007).

Virtually all fee-based financial services are taxable or zero rated under VAT in South Africa. However, margin-based services are still exempted and the banks can reclaim input VAT for fee-based services. In Singapore, financial services rendered to taxable customers are zero rated because financial institutions can claim input credits for VAT. For input VAT that is not attributable to taxable supplies, or to exempt supplies, a financial service provider must allocate the input tax in proportion to the ratio of taxable supplies to total supplies (Schenk and Oldman, 2007).

As noted in Mirrlees et al. (2011), exemption from VAT is against the logic of the tax as it breaks down the chain, leaving financial institutions unable to reclaim the input tax. It is clearly distortionary, as exemption makes VAT a production tax. Perhaps the biggest distortion is that it encourages financial institutions to produce inputs in-house and thus to integrate vertically in order to reduce input VAT that is not creditable for financial institutions. In addition to the discrimination against outside suppliers, vertical integration could perhaps be the reason that financial institutions take the shape of complex conglomerates, making them 'too big to fail'.

Because financial institutions across the EU face different input costs, exemption creates another distortion, leaving the financial institutions with higher input costs uncompetitive.

Another distortion identified by Schenk and Oldman (2007) is that exemption of financial services may encourage financial institutions to outsource overseas, which is discrimination against domestic suppliers. They explain that if a financial institution obtains an exempted service within the EU, the cost may include some disallowed input VAT. However, this is not the case if a service is imported from a country with zero rating on the export of that service.

One of the problems in taxing financial services identified by Benedict (2011) is the valuation issue. Apart from some technical problems involved in it, one factor that is desirable from the risk management point of view is the transparency of banks' earnings. It is generally argued that the tax can be imposed on the interest rate spread and apportioned between the savers and borrowers. This valuation process would result in a transparency of the margins, not only for the revenue authorities but also for the public at large. This would reduce the information asymmetries, which are considered to have been one of the causes of the crisis.

Mirrlees et al. (2010) does not clearly distinguish financial services from other major areas (like property and PNC (public, non-profit and charitable)) where VAT is not optimal because of less than general coverage, less than optimal rate structure and less than perfect administration. Nevertheless, Mirrlees et al. (2010) suggest Viable Integrated VAT (VIVAT) as a solution for the UK and the EU. VIVAT proposes that all sales to registered businesses are taxed at a uniform 'intermediate' rate of 17.5 per cent. However, Cnossen (2010), commenting on Crawford et al.'s chapter on VAT in Mirrlees et al. (2010, Chapter 4), argues that VIVAT involves substantial additional administrative complexity and may violate tax autonomy. It leads to a break in the VAT-audit trail, making it difficult to control compliance. Dickson and White (2010) consider a uniform standard rate of 17.5 per cent a step in the right direction. Given the regressive compliance cost of VAT, they are of the view, because of basic necessities of life, that the economic position of the poor should be adjusted via income taxation and social welfare provisions, rather than VAT exemption.

There are two methods of VAT charging: the subtraction method and the credit-invoice method. The subtraction method exists in Japan, whereas most countries (Europe, Australia, New Zealand, Canada, etc.) use the credit-invoice method. However, Toder and Rosenberg (2010) explain that the subtraction method in Japan is not very different from the credit-invoice method. Under the subtraction method, VAT is calculated on the difference between the value of sales and the value of purchases. On the other hand, in the credit-invoice method, sales by businesses are taxable. However, they reclaim the tax they have paid on their purchases. The credit-invoice method is preferable over the subtraction method if anyone in the chain is exempt from tax. The credit-invoice method is further divided into the cash flow method, cash flow method with tax collection account (TCA), and the modified reverse charge approach.

The cash flow method is more widely used and the simplest method to tackle the valuation of VAT under credit-invoice tax. Under this method, all cash inflows are treated as sales to customers and all cash outflows are treated as the purchase of inputs. Consequently, financial institutions have to pay tax on all purchases (cash outflows) and charge tax on all sales (cash inflows). Financial institutions will reclaim the tax paid on purchases. Although the cash flow method is simple and straightforward to implement, there are two difficulties attached to it, but only for margin-based services. These are related to payment of tax at the time of borrowing and transitional adjustments at the beginning of the system and at the time of tax rate change.

Poddar and English (1997) propose a cash flow method with TCA to resolve the problems attached to this method. They argue that the TCA is a tax suspense account created to obviate the payment of tax by taxpayers and of credits by government during the period that cash inflows and outflows of a capital nature occur.

Tax that would otherwise be payable/creditable is instead debited/credited to the TCA and carried forward to the period during which the capital transaction is reversed. The TCA mechanism thus allows deferral of tax on cash inflows and of tax credits on cash outflows. However, these deferrals are subject to interest charges at the government borrowing rate (Poddar and English, 1997, p. 11).

Zee (2004, p. 3) proposes a modified reverse charge method to tax financial services under a VAT. This proposal involves: the application of a reverse charge that shifts the collection of the VAT on deposit interest from depositors to banks, in conjunction with the establishment of a franking mechanism managed by banks that effectively transfers the VAT so collected to borrowers as credits against the VAT on their loan interest on a transaction-by-transaction basis. The proposal is fully compatible with an invoice-credit VAT and is capable of delivering the correct theoretical result at minimal administrative costs (Zee, 2004, p. 3).

Zee claims that this approach delivers the correct theoretical result but entails minimal administrative costs in terms of either enforcement or compliance. As explained by Kerrigan (2010), both the TCA and the modified reverse charge methods provide a workable solution. However, the TCA method has been field tested with a panel of financial institutions and has been found workable. Therefore, this method is preferred.

Crawford et al. (2010) argue that financial institutions would need to distinguish between registered and non-registered buyers and suggest VIVAT as the best solution for the UK and the EU. Keen (2000) also makes the same argument and compares VIVAT with Compensating VAT (CVAT), explaining that CVAT (which requires sellers to discriminate between buyers located in different provinces of a federation) is designed for countries like Brazil and India where there is a significant central federal tax authority.

The removal of exemption on financial services would mean that in the UK a 20 per cent VAT on financial products and services would be paid by consumers and banks would be allowed to reclaim VAT on inputs, which would reduce their costs. It would also increase revenue for the government. The only affected party in the case of removal of exemption from VAT would be the consumers. It might also improve efficiency because consumers would be discouraged from over-consuming financial services. Zero rating of financial services reduces VAT revenue, but there will be some compensation from increased tax revenue from increased bank profitability of the banks.

It is important to segregate financial services into fee-based services and margin-based services when removing VAT exemption on them. Fee-based services can be categorized as a luxury, with margin-based services as a necessity. Therefore, tax on such services should be levied based on their elasticity of demand. We argued above that raising equity would increase the cost of lending for smaller banks and hence will unfavourably impact them, leaving them at a disadvantage. However, the removal of exemption of VAT would decrease the undue pressure on banks and give them a level playing field, similar to other companies. As highlighted by Mishkin (2012), increased competition, resulting from the financial innovation that decreased the profitability of banks, may have encouraged the excessive risk taking by banks which led to the crisis. We therefore support a combination of both approaches of imposing taxation and new regulations, so that the banks would not be adversely affected by overly strict policies, keeping in mind the tax and regulation heterogeneity that exists across countries and regions.

6.4 A bank levy

A supplementary bank levy, or tax, can be interpreted as an additional duty imposed on financial institutions, predominantly banks. Several countries have taken legislative initiatives in this respect, such as an additional levy applicable to banks that are considered to pose a systemic risk to the economy. Such bank levies are not applied to the profits of the bank (as in the case of CIT), but are in principle levied on its (relevant) assets, liabilities or capital. For example, countries which choose to apply a levy primarily on liabilities include Austria (which also covers some aspects of FTT because the tax is also levied on the volume of derivatives transactions), Belgium (including two other bank taxes explained below), Cyprus, Germany, Hungary, Iceland (which also taxes remuneration in much the same way as an FAT), Portugal, Romania, Slovakia, Sweden, the Netherlands (where the usual rate is multiplied by a factor of 1.1 if one member of the board receives non-fixed remuneration of more than 25 per cent of fixed income), the UK and the US (both the UK and the US give a 50 per cent discount on the usual rate for more stable funding sources). On the other hand, the base of the French bank levy is regulatory capital, while that of Slovenia is total assets.

Some countries, such as the Netherlands, the UK and the US, tax only the banks whose liabilities exceed a certain threshold. For example, there is a threshold of €20 billion in the Netherlands, one of GBP 20 billion in the UK and of US $50 billion in the US. The bank tax in most countries (e.g. Austria, Hungary, France, Iceland, Portugal, Slovakia, Slovenia, the Netherlands and the United Kingdom) contributes to the general reserve; however, there is a dedicated resolution fund to draw upon in case of a crisis in some other countries (e.g. Cyprus, Germany, Korea, Romania and Sweden). In the US, the purpose of the bank tax, called the 'Financial Crisis Responsibility Fee' is different, in the sense that it is ex post and is aimed at recovering any direct costs incurred by the failure of financial institutions under the TARP. Belgium has three different kinds of bank taxes: one similar to the usual bank levies calculated on total liabilities, which contributes to the Resolution Fund; and a bank levy which uses regulated savings deposits as the basis for calculating the tax due, contributing to the deposit protection fund and the financial stability contribution. Finally, there is a contribution to the Special Protection Fund for the deposits, life insurances and capital of recognized cooperative companies, which is calculated taking into account certain risk factors.

Because the Bank Levy is not covered by standard tax treaties, there is a risk of double taxation. In order to avoid this, the UK, German and French authorities are entering into a 'double taxation agreement', which will allow a proportion of the levy in one country to be credited against the levy in the other. This agreement was enacted in the UK with respect to France from 1 January 2011, which allows a proportion of the French levy to be credited against the UK levy.

In the UK, the Chancellor of the Exchequer increased the Bank Levy from 0.105 per cent to 0.13 per cent to 0.142 per cent with effect from 1 January 2014. This is the sixth increase in the levy since it was introduced in 2010. The Government lowered the corporate tax rate from 28 per cent (in April 2010) to 23 per cent (in April 2013) and then to 21 per cent (in April 2014), and it will further decrease to 20 per cent from April 2015. The Bank Levy was increased in order to remove the benefit of this reduction from the banking sector and with a view to raise revenue from it. In the UK, the levy is applicable to global consolidated balance sheet liabilities less Tier 1 capital, protected deposits, sovereign repo liabilities and derivatives on a net basis. Therefore, an increase in the Bank Levy means that the Chancellor is aiming to tax the unsecured borrowings of the banking sector. There seems to be an overlap between the increase in the Bank Levy and the proposed Basel III Liquidity Coverage Ratio (LCR) and Net Stable Funding Ratio (NSFR). The LCR and NSFR incentivize banks to use more stable funding sources by reducing the reliance on short-term wholesale funding. Table 6.3 provides an overview of bank levies around the world.

Table 6.3 Overview of bank levies around the world

| | Bank Definition | Scope | | | | | |
		Domestic Bank (Local Legal Entity)	Foreign Branches of Domestic Bank (Outbounds)	Branches of Foreign Banks (Inbounds)	Branches of EU Passported Banks	Broker Dealers	Non-banking Groups with Bank within Group
Austria Stability levy. Effective from 1 January 2011. Contributes to Treasury	Credit institutions according to the Austrian Banking Act	Yes	May be included	Yes, but the tax is only levied on the branch's adjusted total balance sheet	Yes	Yes, if a credit institution under Austrian regulatory rules	Levy payable by the bank only

Belgium Contribution to the Special Protection Fund for deposits, life insurances and capital of recognized cooperative companies. Effective from 1 January 2012. Contributes to Special Protection Fund	Credit institutions that are established in Belgium. A 'credit institution' is defined as follows: a Belgian or non-resident enterprise of which the professional activities consist of the receiving of deposits or other repayable funds and the granting of credits on its own account, as well as the issuing of payment instruments in the form of electronic money	Yes	Yes	In principle not applicable to foreign branches, except: – for Belgian branches of credit institutions established in other member states of the EEA that have opted to be a facultative member of the Special Protection Fund – for Belgian branches of credit institutions established in non-EEA states that do not currently have in place a deposit protection scheme equivalent to the Belgium scheme	No, other than in the instance of Belgian branches of credit institutions established in other member states of the EEA, that have opted to be a facultative member of the Special Protection Fund	Yes, if fall within the definition of a credit institution	Levy payable by the bank only

Table 6.3 (continued)

| | Bank Definition | Scope | | | | | |
		Domestic Bank (Local Legal Entity)	Foreign Branches of Domestic Bank (Outbounds)	Branches of Foreign Banks (Inbounds)	Branches of EU Passported Banks	Broker Dealers	Non-banking Groups with Bank within Group
Belgium Contribution to the Resolution Fund. Effective from 1 January 2012. Contributes to Resolution Fund	Same definition as that used for contributions to the Special Protection Fund with an exception for institutions for electronic money as given in Title IIbis of the 1993 Law	Yes	Yes	No	No	Yes, if fall within the definition of a credit institution	Levy payable by the bank only

Belgium						
Annual tax on credit institutions (1) Payable yearly on 1 July, and for the first time on 1 July 2012 (2) Please note that we have based our comments regarding this tax on a draft bill that is currently pending and which is not yet approved in Parliament	Credit institutions (same definition as that used for contributions to the Special Protection Fund) that are mentioned on a list of licensed credit institutions made by the Belgian National Bank	Yes	Yes	Yes, applicable to Belgian branches of credit institutions resident in a member state of the EEA. Furthermore, applicable to Belgian branches of credit institutions resident in other states provided that no similar deposit protection system as in Belgium is foreseen	Yes under the same conditions as 'branches of foreign banks'	Yes, if fall within the definition of a credit institution	Levy payable by the bank only

Notes

1. The reason is that corrective taxes need to address the marginal social damage from some activity, which may differ from the average damage.
2. The EC (2010) reports other possibilities, including for instance a surcharge on the rate of corporate income tax applied to financial institutions.
3. It should be noted that the revenue potential of financial transaction taxes will *inter alia* depend on their impact on trading volumes. For the estimates discussed, a 'medium transaction-reduction scenario' is assumed. In that situation, Schulmeister (2011) assumes that the volume of spot transactions in the stock and bond markets would decline by 10 per cent and 5 per cent, respectively. Moreover, the reduction of trading volume of exchange-traded derivatives as well as OTC transactions would lie between 60 and 70 per cent (Schulmeister et al., 2008).
4. A CDS is a swap agreement between the buyer and the seller that the seller of the CDS will compensate the buyer in the event of a loan default (by the debtor). A CDS where the buyer does not own the underlying debt is known as a naked CDS.
5. http://marketsmedia.com/italian-french-trading-volumes-hit-ftt/ dated 23 April 2014, http://www. ftseglobal markets.com/news/ftt-drags-down-italian-stock-trading-volumes.html dated 23 April 2014.
6. See Schamp (2011) for more details.
7. Schwert and Seguin (1993) estimate that a 0.5 per cent Securities Transaction Tax In the US would increase the cost of capital by 10–18 basis points.
8. Although most current proponents of an FTT do not envisage that its base would include current account bank transactions, it is cautionary to recall that while some have advocated this as a relatively progressive form of taxation, such evidence as there is suggests the opposite (Arbelaez et al., 2005).

9. See Schmidt (2007), Schulmeister et al. (2008) and Spratt (2006) for further details.
10. In the case of a turnover tax, tax paid on inputs 'sticks'. However, with VAT, a credit is provided for input tax so as to ensure that, while tax is collected from the seller, it ultimately does not affect businesses' input prices.
11. See Appendix 6 of the IMF (2010) report for an elaboration on the design and revenue potential of these alternative forms of FAT.
12. John et al. (1991) develop the argument for progressive profit taxation on these grounds.
13. Satya and Morley (1997) propose the application of a transaction-based VAT known as the 'Truncated Cash-Flow Method with Tax Calculation Account' as another theoretical possibility. Ernst & Young (1996) has considered such alternative approaches.
14. http://www.hmrc.gov.uk/stats/tax_expenditures/table 1-5.pdf.
15. See GST Guidelines for Working with New Zero Rating Rules for Financial Services, published by policy advice division of the Inland Revenue Department (New Zealand), October 2004.
16. The Value Added Tax Act, no. 89 of 1991 states that various financial services are exempt from VAT, for example long-term insurance (sec. 2(1)(i) and sec. 12(a)). Yet short-term insurance and commission received from selling long-term and short-term insurance are taxable supplies and subject to VAT at 14 per cent.
17. GST/HST Memoranda Series, Canada Customs and Revenue Agency, April 2000.

7. Conclusion and policy recommendations

The optimal combination of regulations and fiscal taxes that would truly circumvent the negative micro-prudential externalities stemming from limited liability and asymmetric information (relating to individual institutions) and macro-prudential externalities relating to systemic risks, remains to be discovered. The impact of these externalities on the growth and development of several countries also remains a source of concern among policy makers, academics, and several national and international bodies. Macro-prudential supervision is an evolving device for reducing asset price inflation, and thus the need to insure against bank failure via capital ratios and deposit insurance and resolution funds, but the proposed macro-prudential policy instruments are untried and untested.

We highlight the inconsistencies within the taxation system and also the inconsistencies between taxation and regulation, with particular focus on banks, and provide an overview of the differing tax regimes between countries.

Current business tax rules arguably encourage excessive leveraging because of the tax deductibility or 'expensing' of interest on debt, in contrast to dividend payments on equity, which are arguably double taxed. Tax expensing should perhaps be removed to give debt equal treatment to equity, at least for banks. However, the increased emphasis on core equity will put the small saving, and particularly mutual, banks at a disadvantage because they cannot issue equity or quasi equity very easily, if at all.

There is concern about the continuing viability of universal banks. The UK's Independent Commission on Banking (ICB, 2011) recommended 'ring fencing' retail banking within universal banks. Ring fencing would impose higher costs on the universal banks and might encourage some of them to divest their retail banking businesses in pursuit of more risky and higher return on equity, generating investment banking and other banking business (Mullineux, 2012). The UK's Parliamentary Commission on Banking Standards (PCBS, 2013a) highlighted that while ring-fenced banks would carry out the majority of their infrastructural economic functions relating to the payments system, which need protecting, it is important to be clear that it is these functions that will enjoy protection, and not the banks, or their shareholders or creditors, other than depositors. There should be no government guarantee for ring-fenced banks, or a perception of one; just depositor protection. Ring fencing does not imply that risks from non-ring-fenced banking activities can be ignored; institutions will remain systemic and difficult to resolve. Based on ICB (2011) and PCBS (2013a) recommendations, the UK passed the Financial Services (Banking Reform) Act (2013). However, the EU is still considering the Liikanen Group (2012) proposals for limited separation of retail and investment banking. With the Volcker Rule passed in the US in 2014 under an amendment to the Dodd–Frank Act (2010), the UK's Prudential Regulatory Authority is to consider such a rule to more severely limit proprietary trading by UK banks and prevent them from running hedge funds. Nevertheless, this is a major ongoing issue, with the big banks lobbying hard for a relaxation in the constraints.

In 2014, the UK Treasury increased the Bank Levy for a sixth time since it was introduced in 2010 in order to compensate for the benefits banks enjoy from the falling corporate tax rate. The initial purpose of the Bank Levy was to tax the unsecured borrowings of the banking sector while forcing banks to contribute to the fiscal consolidation their failures had made necessary. Since the objective of the Basel III Liquidity Coverage Ratio and Net Stable Funding Ratio is also to reduce reliance on short-term borrowings, there is potential overlap. As the stock of non-core liabilities reflects the under-pricing of risk in the financial system, we are of the view that a (risk-related) levy on non-core liabilities may perhaps mitigate the distortions. Further progress was made towards an EU Banking Union following an agreement on 18 December 2013, which included a proposal to use a bank levy to build up, over a number of years, a Bank Resolution and Recovery Fund to protect against the need for taxpayer-funded bank bail-outs. We propose that the UK use its Bank Levy to take similar action.

The literature reporting on the empirical analysis of the effects of an FTT, which involves a fixed levy on the value of a currency or a financial asset (e.g. shares) traded, finds that it can be distortionary, as it reduces market trading volume and liquidity, and increases market volatility and cost of capital for firms. There is also the risk of a double 'taxation' of liquidity: once via an FTT and then from the higher liquidity reserve requirements under Basel III. To assure market liquidity, ideally there should be large numbers of buyers and sellers of an asset. Because Basel III requires banks to hold more liquidity on their balance sheets, it will decrease the number of buyers in the market, and this situation could cause difficulties in times when many banks are seeking to sell their liquid assets following a major event, leading to 'fire sale' losses or a breakdown in interbank lending as in the August 2007 North Atlantic Liquidity Squeeze. If an FTT is to be implemented, then its level should be carefully calibrated.

Under Basel III and at the instigation of the Financial Stability Board (FSB, 2014), banks must also hold more capital to absorb losses, making them less risky. Their increased Total Loss Absorbing Capacity (TLAC) makes them less risky, which should make it cheaper for them to raise capital and so they may not necessarily lend significantly less (Admati and Hellwig, 2013). Furthermore, if the tax distortions favouring debt over equity are redressed or reversed, with perhaps a bias towards equity instead, the higher regulatory capital ratios need not lead to lower bank lending in 'normal' times. Further, the return on equity expected by institutional investors in banks was arguably excessive ahead of the crisis. Shifting the emphasis towards return on assets is recommended as an alternative. To the extent that an FTT leads to an increased cost of the raising capital, it might offset some of these benefits, but then the costs may be passed on to other market participants by the banks.

There is a fear that the proposed EU FTT might adversely impact the repo market, which is already being undermined by the Volcker Rule in the US. Because central banks use the repo rate as a key monetary policy instrument, a substantial increase in the cost of repo transactions would require alternative monetary policy tools to be developed, and there is evidence that this may be required as 'Quantitative Easing' is unwound anyway. However, it might also substantially increase the cost of liquidity management for other market participants.

The originally proposed EU FTT is applicable to other non-participating member countries and to third countries if they are counterparty to financial transaction trading in an FTT zone jurisdiction, and in the UK transactions might be subject to both UK stamp duty and the EU FTT, so there is clearly a risk of double taxation for non-participating member countries. Moreover, the 2010 Mirrlees Review of the UK tax system and the 2010 Henry Review of the Australian tax system warn against the distortionary effects of transaction taxes in general. Are there better alternatives and should a low-level FTT, at least on equity trading, be used to discourage over-trading and short termism as proposed by Tobin (1984)?

Financial services are currently 'exempt' from VAT in the EU, including the UK. Hence, banks cannot reclaim input VAT paid on their purchases relative to other firms.

The removal of the exemption of VAT on financial services and the segregation of fee-based services and interest margin-based services is proposed. Removal of the exemption would increase revenue for the government, but consumers would be liable to pay additional taxes on the use of financial services. This might increase efficiency because it would discourage wasteful use of these services and eliminate the distortionary cross-subsidization that underpins 'free banking' in the UK. Furthermore, it would reduce the incentive for vertical integration in financial institutions to avoid paying VAT that cannot be claimed to suppliers, which reinforces their 'bigness' and complexity in banking. Given the operational difficulties linked to the removal of exemption from VAT, the cash flow method with a Tax Collection Account proposed by Poddar and English (1997) is recommended. It should be noted that the more recently developed value added-based GST systems in Australia, and especially New Zealand, raise (proportionally, given their lower tax rates) considerably more revenues from taxing financial goods and services.

Because of particular operational difficulties associated with levying VAT on interest margin-based financial services, as opposed to fee-based service provision, an FAT is sometimes recommended as an alternative solution. An FAT is a tax on aggregate bonuses plus profits of a banking firm, which is equivalent to aggregate 'value added'. An FAT might be preferred over an FTT because it is less easily avoided through choice of geographic location, its incidence is more certain and it would generate fewer distortions. An FAT is also considered to be a broad 'net' measure of a VAT, compared with an FTT's narrow 'gross' measure of financial sector activity, and has the potential advantage of taxing the bonus pool. It does not, however, have the potentiality to affect consumer behaviour beneficially, in the way that a VAT levied directly on financial products and services might have, or to discourage over-trading and short termism, as an FTT might do.

The importance of international cooperation has never been so clear, given the externalities and the potentiality for international 'spillovers' involved in globalized financial markets. Not only must regulation and supervision be uniformly applied to achieve a 'level playing field', but financial, and other, taxes need to be harmonized to a much greater extent to reduce the incentive for regulatory and other tax arbitrage. This will become all the more important as attention switches to domestically oriented 'macroprudential' tools, or 'taxes'.

The Financial Services Board, which is leading the drive for international coordination, is well aware the reforms need to be carefully designed so as not to hinder the banking sector's ability to increase TLAC, and to ensure that 'shadow banking' is not unduly advantaged by 'over-regulating' or 'over-taxing' banks. With this in mind, the FSB (2013) introduced 'haircuts' on stock lending for repos to limit the build-up of excessive leverage outside the banking system, which may also reduce procyclicality of that leverage, and there have been moves to enhance the capital adequacy of money market mutual funds (FSOC, 2012).

The overall message seems to be that the focus should shift to taxing banking, rather than banks *per se*, and wider financial activities, goods and services, as well as profits and bonuses. Additionally, pooled insurance solutions with risk-related premiums (or 'taxes') should be sought to protect deposits and liquidity, requiring a re-definition of conditions for access to central bank liquidity provision, so that individual banks do not need to hold unnecessarily excessive in-house reserves. Bank regulatory and tax systems are advancing gradually, but there is much yet to be done and the globalization of finance requires substantial international cooperation which will be severely tested in the event of the need for the resolution of a major international bank.

References

Acharya, V., Pedersen, L., Phillippon, T. and Richardson, M. (2010). 'Measuring Systemic Risk.' *Working Paper No. 1002*, Federal Reserve Bank of Cleveland.

Admati, A. and Hellwig, M. (2013). *The Bankers' New Clothes – What's Wrong with Banking and What to do About It.* Princeton: Princeton University Press.

Adrian, T. and Brunnermeier, M. (2011). 'CoVaR.' Staff Reports 348, New York: Federal Reserve Bank of New York.

Amihud, Y. and Mendelson, H. (1992). 'Transaction Taxes and Stock Values.' In K. Lehn and R. Kamphuis (eds), *Modernizing U.S. Securities Regulation: Economic and Legal Perspective*, pp. 477–500. Chicago: Irwin Professional Publishing.

Arbelaez, M., Leonard, B. and Zuluaga, S. (2005). 'The Bank Debit Tax in Colombia.' In R.M. Bird, J.M. Poterba and J. Slemrod (eds), *Fiscal Reform in Colombia*. Cambridge: MIT Press.

Atkinson, A.B. and Stiglitz, J.E. (1976). 'The Design of Tax Structure: Direct Versus Indirect Taxation.' *Journal of Public Economics*, 6(1–2): 55–75.

Auerbach, A.J. and Gordon, R.H. (2002). 'Taxation of Financial Services Under a VAT.' *American Economic Review*, 92(2): 411–416.

Bagehot, W. (1873). *Lombard Street: A Description of the Money Market*. London: King; reprinted New York: Wiley, 1999. Accessed 27 March 2015 via http://www.gutenberg.org/ebooks/4359?msg=welcome_stranger.

Baltagi, B.H., Li, D. and Li, Q. (2006). 'Transaction Tax and Stock Market Behaviour: Evidence from an Emerging Market.' *Empirical Economics*, 31(2): 393–408.

Bank of England (2009). *The Role of Macroeconomics Policy: A Discussion Paper*. London: Bank of England. Accessed 27 March 2015 via http://www.bankofengland.co.uk/publications/Documents/other/financialstability/roleofmacroprudentialpolicy091121.pdf.

Becchetti, L., Ferrari, M. and Trenta, U. (2013). 'The Impact of the French Tobin Tax.' *CEIS Working Paper No. 266*, Centre for Economic and International Studies.

Benedict, K. (2011). 'The Australian GST Regime and Financial Services: How Did We Get Here and Where Are We Going?' *eJournal of Tax Research*, 9(2): 174–193.

Bernanke, B.S. and Gertler, M. (1995). 'Inside the Black Box: The Credit Channel of Monetary Policy Transmission.' *Journal of Economic Perspectives*, 9(4): 27–48.

BIS (2010). *80th Annual Report. 28 June 2010.* Basel: Bank for International Settlements.

BIS (2011). *Basel III: A Global Regulatory Framework for More Resilient Banks and Banking Systems.* Basel: Bank for International Settlements.

Bloomfield, R., O'Hara, M. and Saar, G. (2009). 'How Noise Trading Affects Markets: An Experimental Analysis.' *Review of Financial Studies*, 22(6): 2275–2302.

Boadway, R. and Keen, M. (2003). 'Theoretical Perspectives on the Taxation of Capital Income and Financial Services.' In P. Honohan, (ed.), *Taxation of Financial Intermediation*, pp. 31–80. New York: World Bank and Oxford University Press.

Bodie, Z., Kane, A. and Marcus, A. (2013). *Investments*. New York: McGraw-Hill Higher Education, 9th Edition.

Bond, S., Hawkins, M. and Klemm, A. (2004). 'Stamp Duty on Shares and its Effect on Share Prices.' *IFS Working Paper No. W04/11*, Institute for Fiscal Studies.

Brunnermeier, M.K., Crocket, A., Goodhart, C., Persaud, A. and Shin, H. (2009). *The Fundamental Principles of Financial Regulation*. Geneva Reports on the World Economy 11. Geneva: International Center for Monetary and Banking Studies.

Calomiris, C. (2013). 'Should Big Banks Be Broken Up?' *The Economist*. Accessed 27 March 2015 via http://www.economist.com/debate/days/view/977.

Capelle-Blancard, G. (2014). 'Securities Transaction Tax in Europe: First Impact Assessment.' In S. Chaudhry and A. Mullineux (eds), *Taxing Banks Fairly*, pp. 107–126. Cheltenham, UK and Northampton, MA, USA: Edward Elgar.

Capelle-Blancard, G. and Havrylchyk, O. (2013). 'The Impact of the French Securities Transaction Tax on Market Liquidity and Volatility.' *CES Working Paper*, Centre d'Economie de la Sorbonne.

Cecchetti, S.G., Kohler, M. and Upper, C. (2009). *Financial Crisis and Economic Activity. Financial Stability and Macroeconomic Policy*. Kansas City: Federal Reserve Bank of Kanas City.

Ceriani, V., Manestra, S., Ricotti, G., Sanelli, A. and Zangari, E. (2011). 'The Tax System and the Financial Crisis.' *Occasional Paper No. 85*, Banca d'Italia.

Cnossen, S. (2010). 'Commentary on I. Crawford, M. Keen and S. Smith, "Value Added Tax and Excises."' In J. Mirrlees, S. Adam, T. Besley, R. Blundell, S. Bond, R. Chote, M. Gammie, P. Johnson, G. Myles and J. Poterba (eds), *Dimensions of Tax Design: The Mirrlees Review*, pp. 370–386. Oxford: Institute for Fiscal Studies.

Colliard, J. and Hoffmann, P. (2013). 'Sand in the Chips: Evidence on Taxing Transactions in an Electronic Market.' *Mimeo*. Frankfurt: European Central Bank.

Corlett, W. and Hague, D. (1953). 'Complementarity and the Excess Burden of Taxation.' *Review of Economic Studies*, 21: 21–30.

Cortez, B. and Vogel, T. (2011). 'A Financial Transaction Tax for Europe.' *EC Tax Review*, 20(1): 16–29.

Coulter, B., Mayer, C. and Vickers, J. (2013). 'Taxation and Regulation of Banks to Manage Systemic Risk.' *Finance Working Paper No. 341/ 2013*, European Corporate Governance Institute.

Crawford, I., Keen, M. and Smith, S. (2010). 'Value Added Tax and Excises.' In J. Mirrlees, S. Adam, T. Besley, R. Blundell, S. Bond, R. Chote, M. Gammie, P. Johnson, G. Myles and J. Poterba (eds), *Dimensions of Tax Design: The Mirrlees Review*, pp. 275–362. Oxford: Institute for Fiscal Studies.

Crockett, A. (2000). *Marrying the Micro- and Macro-prudential Dimensions of Financial Stability*. Basel: Bank for International Settlements, Financial Stability Forum.

CRPMG (2008). *Containing Systemic Risk: The Road to Reform*. Report of the Counterparty Risk Management Policy Group/CRPMG III, 6 August 2008. Accessed 27 March 2015 via http://www.crmpolicygroup.org/docs/CRMP G-III.pdf.

De Larosière, J. (2009). *The High Level Group on Financial Supervision in the EU*. Brussels: European Commission

De Mooij, R., Keen, M. and Orihara, M. (2013). 'Taxation, Bank Leverage, and Financial Crises.' *IMF Working Paper, WP/13/48*, International Monetary Fund.

De Nicolò, G., Gamba, A. and Lucchetta, M. (2012). 'Capital Regulation, Liquidity Requirements and Taxation in a Dynamic Model of Banking.' *IMF Working Paper, WP/12/72*, International Monetary Fund.

Dickson, I. and White, D. (2010). 'Commentary on I. Crawford, M. Keen and S. Smith, "Value Added Tax and Excises."' In J. Mirrlees, S. Adam, T. Besley, R. Blundell, S. Bond, R. Chote, M. Gammie, P. Johnson, G. Myles and J. Poterba (eds), *Dimensions of Tax Design: The Mirrlees Review*, pp. 387–406. Oxford: Institute for Fiscal Studies.

Dickson, I. and White, D. (2012). 'Tax Design Insights from the New Zealand Goods and Services Tax (GST) Model.' *Working Paper No. 60*, Working Papers Series,Victoria University of Wellington.

Dodd–Frank Act (2010). 'Dodd–Frank Wall Street Reform and Consumer Protection Act.' *111th Congress Public Law 203*. Accessed 27 March 2015 via http://www.gpo.gov/fdsys/pkg/PLAW-111publ203/html/PLAW-111publ203.htm.

EC (2010). 'Taxation Papers: Financial Sector Taxation.' *Working Paper No. 25*, European Commission.

EC (2011). *Proposal for a Council Directive on a Common System of Financial Transaction Tax and Amending Directive 2008/7/EC.* Report, Brussels: European Commission.

Egger, P.H., Ehrlich, M. and Radulescu, D. (2012). 'How Much it Pays to Work in the Financial Sector.' *CESifo Economic Studies*, 58(1): 110–139.

Engel, E., Erickson, M. and Maydew, E. (1999). 'Debt Equity Hybrid Securities.' *Journal of Accounting Research*, 37(2): 249–274.

Ernst & Young (1996). 'Value Added Tax: A Study of Methods of Taxing Financial and Insurance Services.' *Taxation Studies 0002*, Directorate General Taxation and Customs Union. Brussels: European Commission.

Federal Reserve Board. (2014). Volcker Rule Amendment. Accessed 27 March 2015 via http://www.federalreserve.gov/newsevents/press/other/20141028a.htm.

Firth, M. and McKenzie, K. (2012). 'The GST and Financial Services: Pausing for Perspective.' *SPP Research Papers* 29. Calgary: University of Calgary.

FSB (2011). *Policy Measures to Address Systemically Important Financial Institutions.* Basel: Financial Stability Board. Accessed 27 March 2015 via http://www.financialstabilityboard.org/publications/r_111104bb.pdf.

FSB (2013). *Strengthening Oversight and Regulation of Shadow Banking.* Basel: Financial Stability Board. Accessed 27 March 2015 via http://

www.financialstabilityboard.org/wp-content/
uploads/r_130829b.pdf?page_moved=1.

FSB (2014). *Adequacy of Loss-Absorbing Capacity of Global Systemically Important Banks in Resolution*. Basel: Financial Stability Board. Accessed 27 March 2015 via http://www.financial stabilityboard.org/wp- content/uploads/tlac-condoc-6-nov-2014-final.pdf.

FSOC (2012). *Proposed Recommendations Regarding Money Market Mutual Fund Reform* (November 2012). Washington: Financial Stability Oversight Council. Accessed 27 March 2015 via http://www.treasury.gov/initiatives/fsoc/Documents/Proposed%20Recommendations%20Regarding%20Money%20Market%20Mutual%20Fund%20Reform%20-%20November%2013,%202012.pdf.

Gaston, E. and Song, I. (2014). 'Supervisory Roles in Loan Loss Provisioning in Countries Implementing IFRS.' *IMF Working Papers WP/14/170*, International Monetary Fund.

Genser, B. and Winker, P. (1997). 'Measuring the Fiscal Revenue Loss of VAT Exemption in Commercial Banking.' *Public Finance Analysis*, 54(4): 563–585.

Gibbons, D. (2014). *Britain's Personal Debt Crisis: How We Got Here and What To Do About It*. Coventry: Searching Finance Ltd.

Grubert, H. and Mackie, J.B. (2000). 'Must Financial Services Be Taxed Under a Consumption Tax?' *National Tax Journal*, 53(1): 23–40.

Haferkorn, M. and Zimmermann, K. (2013). 'Securities Transaction Tax and Market Quality: The Case of France.' *Mimeo*. Frankfurt: Goethe University.

Hanson, S., Kashyap, A. and Stein, J. (2011). 'A Macroprudential Approach to Financial Regulation.' *Journal of Economic Perspectives*, 25(1): 3–28.

Hart, O. and Zingales, L. (2009). 'To Regulate Finance: Try the Market.' *Foreign Policy*. Accessed 27 March 2015 via http://experts. foreignpolicy.com/posts/2009/03/30/to_regu late_finance_try_the_market.

Hemmelgarn, T. and Nicodeme, G. (2010). 'The 2008 Financial Crisis and Taxation Policy.' *Taxation Papers Working Paper No. 20 2010*, European Commission – Directorate General for Taxation and Customs Union.

Hemmelgarn, T., Nicodeme, G. and Zangari, E. (2011). 'The Role of Housing Tax Provisions in the 2008 Financial Crisis.' *Taxation Papers 27*. Brussels: European Commission – Directorate General Taxation and Customs Union.

Henry, K. (2010). 'Australia's Future Tax System.' *Report to the Treasurer, Commonwealth of Australia*. Accessed 27 March 2015 via http:// www.ag.gov.ua/cca.

Hines, J.R. and Hubbard, R.G. (1990). 'Coming Home to America: Dividend Repatriation by U.S. Multinationals.' In A. Razin and R.G. Hubbard (eds), *Taxation in the Global Economy*. Chicago: University of Chicago Press.

HKMA (2013). *2013 Annual Report*. Hong Kong: Hong Kong Monetary Authority.

HM Treasury (2010). *Final Legislation on the Bank Levy*. London: HM Treasury. Accessed 27 March 2015 via https://www.gov.uk/government/news/government-publishes-final-legislation-on-the-bank-levy.

Huizinga, H. (2002). 'A European VAT on Financial Services?' *Economic Policy*, 17(35): 499–534.

ICB (2011). *Final Report Recommendations*. London: Independent Commission on Banking. Accessed 27 March 2015 via http://www. parliament.uk/business/committees/committees-a-z/commons-select/treasury-committee/inquiries1/icb-final-report/.

IMF (2009). *Debt Bias and Other Distortions: Crisis-related Issues in Tax Policy*. Fiscal Affairs Department, Washington: International Monetary Fund.

IMF (2010). *A Fair and Substantial Contribution by the Financial Sector: Final Report for the G-20*. Washington: International Monetary Fund.

IMF (2014a). *World Economic Outlook: Recovery Strengthens, Remains Uneven*. April. Washington: International Monetary Fund.

IMF (2014b). *Fiscal Monitor: Public Expenditure Reform, Making Difficult Choices*. April. Washington: International Monetary Fund.

IMF (2014c). *Global Financial Stability Report: Moving from Liquidity- to Growth-Driven Markets*. April. Washington: International Monetary Fund.

John, K., John T. and Senbet, L. (1991). 'Risk-Shifting Incentives of Depository Institutions: A New Perspective on Federal Deposit Insurance Reform.' *Journal of Banking and Finance*, 15: 895–915.

Jones, C.M. and Seguin, P.J. (1997). 'Transaction Costs and Price Volatility: Evidence from Commission Deregulation.' *American Economic Review*, 87(4): 728–737.

Keen, M. (2000). 'VIVAT, CVAT, and All That – New Forms of Value-Added Tax for Federal Systems.' *IMF Working Papers WP/00/83*, International Monetary Fund.

Keen, M. (2011). 'Rethinking the Taxation of the Financial Sector.' *CESifo Economic Studies*, 57(1): 1–24.

Kerrigan, A. (2010). 'The Elusiveness of Neutrality. Why is it So Difficult to Apply VAT to Financial Services?' *MPRA Paper 22748*, University of Munich.

Klein, N. (2014). 'Small and Medium Size Enterprises, Credit Supply Shocks, and Economic Recovery in Europe.' *IMF Working Papers WP/14/98*, International Monetary Fund.

Klemm, A. (2007). 'Allowances for Corporate Equity in Practice.' *CESifo Economic Studies*, 53(2): 229–262.

KPMG (2012). 'Bank Levies – Comparison of Certain Jurisdictions.' *Report*, International, Edition IX, June.

Laeven, L. and Valencia, F. (2010). 'Systemic Banking Crisis: The New and the Old, the

Good and the Ugly.' *IMF Working Paper, WP/10/146*, International Monetary Fund.

Liikanen Group (2012). *Report of the European Commission's High-Level Expert Group on Bank Structural Reform*, 9 October. Accessed 27 March 2015 via www.ec.europa.eu.

Lockwood, B. (2010). 'How Should Financial Intermediation Services be Taxed?' *Warwick Economic Research Papers*, Department of Economics, University of Warwick.

Luttrell, D., Atkinson, T. and Rosenblum, H. (2013). 'Assessing the Costs and Consequences of the 2007–09 Financial Crisis and Its Aftermath.' *Dallas Fed Economic Letter*, 8(7).

Meyer, S., Wagner, M. and Weinhardt, C. (2013). 'Politically Motivated Taxes in Financial Markets: The Case of the French Financial Transaction Tax.' *Mimeo*. Stuttgart Stock Exchange and Karlsruhe Institute of Technology.

Mian, A. and Sufi, A. (2014). *House of Debt: How They (and You) Caused the Great Recession, and How We Can Prevent it from Happening Again*. Chicago: The University of Chicago Press.

Mirrlees, J., Adam, S., Besley, T., Blundell, R., Bond, S., Chote, R., Gammie, M., Johnson, P., Myles, G. and Poterba, J. (eds) (2010). *Dimensions of Tax Design: The Mirrlees Review*. Oxford: Oxford University Press.

Mirrlees, J., Adam, S., Besley, T., Blundell, R., Bond, S., Chote, R., Gammie, M., Johnson, P.,

Myles, G. and Poterba, J. (2011). *Tax by Design: The Mirrlees Review.* Oxford: Oxford University Press.

Mishkin, F. (2012). *Economics of Money, Banking, and Financial Markets.* (10th edition) New York: Prentice Hall.

Modigliani, F. and Miller, M. (1958). 'The Cost of Capital, Corporation Finance and the Theory of Investment.' *American Economic Review,* 48(3): 261–297.

Mullineux, A.W. (2012). 'Taxing Banks Fairly.' *International Review of Financial Analysis,* 25: 154–158.

Mullineux, A.W. (2013). 'Banking for the Public Good.' *International Review of Financial Analysis.* Accessed 27 March 2015 via http://dx.doi. org/10.1016/j.irfa.2013.11.001.

Mullineux, A.W. (2014). 'Have We Made Banking Good?' *Working Paper, BURO,* Bournemouth University.

Nocera, J. (2009). 'Risk Management'. *New York Times.* Accessed 27 March 2015 via http://www. nytimes.com/2009/01/04/magazine/04risk-t. html?pagewanted=all&_r=0.

OECD (2007). *Fundamental Reform of Corporate Income Tax.* Paris: Organization for Economic Co-operation and Development.

Parwada, J.T., Rui, Y. and Shen, J. (2013). 'Financial Transaction Tax and Market Quality: Evidence from the French FTT Regulation in 2012.', Social Sciences Research Network, November.

PCBS (2013a). *Changing Banking for Good*. London: Parliamentary Commission on Banking Standards. Accessed 27 March 2015 via http://www.parliament.uk/business/committees/committees-a-z/joint-select/professional-standards-in-the-banking-industry/news/changing-banking-for-good-report/.

PCBS (2013b). *Panel on Tax, Audit and Accounting*. London: Parliamentary Commission on Banking Standards, A Joint Committee of the House of Commons and the House of Lords.

Perotti, E. and Suarez, J. (2009). 'Liquidity Risk Charges as a Macroprudential Tool.' *CEPR Polity Insight No. 40*, Center for Economic Policy Research.

Philippon, T. and Reshef, A. (2009). 'Wages and Human Capital in the U.S. Financial Industry: 1999–2006.' *NBER Working Paper No. 14644*, National Bureau of Economic Research.

Poddar, S. and English, M. (1997). 'Taxation of Financial Services Under a Value-Added Tax: Applying the Cash-Flow Approach.' *National Tax Journal*, 50(1): 89–111.

Poddar, S. and Kalita, J. (2010). 'Treatment of Financial Services under the UAE VAT.' In E. Ahmad and A. Al Faris (eds), *Fiscal Reforms in the Middle East: VAT in the Gulf Cooperation Council*, pp. 256–280. Cheltanham, UK and Northampton, MA, USA: Edward Elgar.

Pomeranets, A. and Weaver, D.G. (2011). 'Security Transaction Taxes and Market Quality.' *Working Papers 11–26*, Bank of Canada.

Pricen, S. (2010). *How Does a Tax Allowance for Corporate Equity Affect Capital Structure? An Empirical Evaluation.* Master's thesis. Louvain: Louvain School of Management.

PWC (2006). *Economic Effects of the VAT Exemption for Financial and Insurance Services.* Report to the European Commission. Brussels: Pricewater-houseCoopers.

Rajan, R. (2011). 'Some Thoughtful Criticism and a Response.' Fault Lines Official Blog, 25 January. Accessed 27 March 2015 via http:// forums.chicagobooth.edu/faultlines?entry=29.

Samuelson, P. (1954). 'The Pure Theory of Public Expenditure.' *Review of Economics and Statistics*, 36(4): 387–389.

Satya, P. and Morley, E. (1997). 'Taxation of Financial Services under a Value-Added Tax: Applying the Cash Flow Approach.' *National Tax Journal*, 50(1): 89–112.

Schamp, L. (2011). *The Challenge of Designing a Financial Sector Tax.* Maastricht: Maastricht University.

Schenk, A.S. (2010). 'Taxation of Financial Services (Including Insurance) Under a U.S. Value-Added Tax.' *Tax Law Review*, 63(2): 409–442.

Schenk, A.S. and Oldman, O. (2007). *Value Added Tax: A Comparative Approach.* New York: Cambridge University Press.

Schmidt, R. (2007). *The Currency Transaction Tax: Rate and Revenue Estimates.* Ontario: The North–South Institute.

Schulmeister, S. (2011). *A General Financial Trans-action Tax. Motives, Revenues, Feasibility and Effects*. Brussels: Brussels Tax Forum, 28 and 29 March.

Schulmeister, S., Schratzenstaller, M. and Picek, O. (2008). 'A General Financial Transaction Tax. Motives, Revenues, Feasibility and Effects.' *Working Paper Series*, Austrian Institute of Economic Research.

Schwert, G.W. and Seguin, P.J. (1993). 'Securities Transaction Taxes: An Overview of Costs, Benefits and Unsolved Questions.' *Financial Analyst Journals*, 49: 27–35.

SEC (2013). *Volcker-Type Rule*. Report, U.S. Securities and Exchange Commission, Washington. Accessed 27 March 2015 via http://www.sec.gov/rules/final/2013/bhca-1.pdf.

Shaviro, D. (2011). 'The 2008 Financial Crisis: Implications for Income Tax Reform.' *Report 09-35*, NYU Law and Economics Research Paper.

Shaviro, D. (2012). 'The Financial Transactions Tax versus the Financial Activities Tax.' *Report 12-04*, NYU Law and Economics Research Paper.

Shin, H. (2011). 'Macroprudential Policies Beyond Basel III.' In Bank for International Settlements (ed.), *Macroprudential Regulation and Policy*, Volume 60 of BIS Papers, pp. 5–15. Basel: Bank for International Settlements.

Smith, A. (1776). *An Inquiry into the Nature and Causes of the Wealth of Nations*. An Electronic

Classics Series Publication. Accessed 27 March 2015 via http://www2.hn.psu.edu/faculty/jmanis/adam-smith/wealth-nations.pdf.

Spratt, S. (2006). *A Sterling Solution: Implementing a Stamp Duty on Sterling to Finance International Development.* A Report for Stamp Out Poverty. London: Intelligence Capital Limited.

Staderini, A. (2001). 'Tax Reforms to Influence Corporate Financial Policy: The Case of the Italian Business Tax Reform of 1997–98.' *Working Paper No. 423*, Banca d'Italia.

Taleb, N.N. (2010). *The Black Swan: The Impact of the Highly Improbable.* (2nd edition). New York: Random House Publishing Group.

Tobin, J. (1978). 'A Proposal for International Monetary Reform.' *Eastern Economic Journal*, 153–159.

Tobin, J. (1984). 'On the Efficiency of the Financial System.' *Lloyds Bank Review*, July: 1–15.

Toder, E. and Rosenberg, J. (2010). *Effects of Imposing a Value-Added Tax to Replace Payroll Taxes or Corporate Taxes.* Washington: Tax Policy Centre, Urban Institute and Brookings Institution.

UK Parliament (2013). 'Financial Services (Banking Reform) Act.' Accessed 27 March 2015 via http://www.legislation.gov.uk/ukpga/2013/33/pdfs/ukpga_20130033_en.pdf.

Umlauf, S.R. (1993). 'Transaction Taxes and the Behaviour of the Swedish Stock Market.' *Journal of Financial Economics*, 33(2): 227–240.

UN (2010). *Report of the Secretary-General's High-Level Advisory Group on Climate Change Financing*. New York: United Nations Framework Convention on Climate Change.

Weichenrieder, A. and Klautke, T. (2008). 'Taxes and the Efficiency Costs of Capital Distortions.' *CESifo Working Paper No. 2431*, Leibniz Institute for Economic Research at the University of Munich.

Weitzman, M. (1974). 'Prices Versus Quantities.' *Review of Economic Studies*, 41(4): 477–491.

Zee, H.H. (2004). 'A New Approach to Taxing Financial Intermediation Services Under a Value-Added Tax.' *IMF Working Paper, WP/04/119*, International Monetary Fund.

Index